PEOPLE
IN THE NEWS

Tim Allen

by Terri Dougherty

**LUCENT
BOOKS** ®

THOMSON
————✶————™
GALE

San Diego • Detroit • New York • San Francisco • Cleveland
New Haven, Conn. • Waterville, Maine • London • Munich

THOMSON

GALE™

For my dad, husband, and son, who are handy to have around, and my mom and daughters, who know the value of reading the directions.

LIBRARY OF CONGRESS CATALOGING-IN-PUBLICATION DATA

Dougherty, Terri.
    Tim Allen / by Terri Dougherty.
    p. cm. — (People in the news)
Summary: A biography of the star of the television show "Home Improvement," discussing his early life, time in prison, career as a comedian, and success in both television and the movies.
Includes bibliographical references and index.
    ISBN 1-59018-241-3
    1. Allen, Tim, 1953– Juvenile literature. 2. Television actors and actresses—United States—Biography—Juvenile literature. 3. Comedians—United States—Biography—Juvenile literature. 4. Allen, Tim, 1953– [1. Actors and actresses. 2. Comedians.]
I. Title. II. People in the news (San Diego, Calif.)
    PN2287.A488 D68 2003
    791.45′028′092—dc21
                                                            2002009881

Printed in the United States of America

Table of Contents

Foreword

FAME AND CELEBRITY are alluring. People are drawn to those who walk in fame's spotlight, whether they are known for great accomplishments or for notorious deeds. The lives of the famous pique public interest and attract attention, perhaps because their experiences seem in some ways so different from, yet in other ways so similar to, our own.

Newspapers, magazines, and television regularly capitalize on this fascination with celebrity by running profiles of famous people. For example, television programs such as *Entertainment Tonight* devote all of their programming to stories about entertainment and entertainers. Magazines such as *People* fill their pages with stories of the private lives of famous people. Even newspapers, newsmagazines, and television news frequently delve into the lives of well-known personalities. Despite the number of articles and programs, few provide more than a superficial glimpse at their subjects.

Lucent's People in the News series offers young readers a deeper look into the lives of today's newsmakers, the influences that have shaped them, and the impact they have had in their fields of endeavor and on other people's lives. The subjects of the series hail from many disciplines and walks of life. They include authors, musicians, athletes, political leaders, entertainers, entrepreneurs, and others who have made a mark on modern life and who, in many cases, will continue to do so for years to come.

These biographies are more than factual chronicles. Each book emphasizes the contributions, accomplishments, or deeds that have brought fame or notoriety to the individual and shows how that person has influenced modern life. Authors portray their subjects in a realistic, unsentimental light. For example, Bill Gates—the cofounder and chief executive officer of the software giant Microsoft—has been instrumental in making personal computers the most vital tool of the modern age. Few dispute his business savvy, his perseverance, or his technical expertise, yet critics say he is ruthless in his dealings with competitors and driven more by his desire to maintain Microsoft's dominance in the computer industry than by an interest in furthering technology.

In these books, young readers will encounter inspiring stories about real people who achieved success despite enormous obstacles. Oprah Winfrey—the most powerful, most watched, and wealthiest woman on television today—spent the first six years of her life in the care of her grandparents while her unwed mother sought work and a better life elsewhere. Her adolescence was colored by promiscuity, pregnancy at age fourteen, rape, and sexual abuse.

Each author documents and supports his or her work with an array of primary and secondary source quotations taken from diaries, letters, speeches, and interviews. All quotes are footnoted to show readers exactly how and where biographers derive their information and provide guidance for further research. The quotations enliven the text by giving readers eyewitness views of the life and accomplishments of each person covered in the People in the News series.

In addition, each book in the series includes photographs, annotated bibliographies, timelines, and comprehensive indexes. For both the casual reader and the student researcher, the People in the News series offers insight into the lives of today's newsmakers—people who shape the way we live, work, and play in the modern age.

Introduction

Toolin' Around

Iт was a quintessential Tim Allen moment.

At home with his wife, he decided to fix a portable light that had been acting up. Figuring that a wire was loose, Allen slowly took it apart. His wife, watching nearby, was fairly certain that he didn't have a clue as to how to fix it. "You sure you know what you're doing?"[1] she asked.

Allen forged ahead confidently. After working on the light and thinking all was well, he plugged the unit back into the wall. However, he forgot he was still holding two wires. The electrical shock sent him rocketing across the kitchen. As he sat stunned on the kitchen floor, his wife remained unaffected by his brush with the electrical current. She simply said, "I told you you didn't know what you were doing."[2]

Allen's home repair mishap could have been a scene from his *Home Improvement* television show or a bit from his stand-up routine. Home repairs and family relationships have been the cornerstone of Allen's career as a comedian, actor, and writer. He has figured out how to get laughs out of power tools, floor drains, and riding lawn mowers.

Yet Allen's real life hasn't been as neat and tidy as one would expect from his reputation as a family entertainment icon. He projects a wholesome paternal image in his television show and movies like *The Santa Clause,* but he got his start in the entertainment industry as a stand-up comic whose dirty humor wasn't suited at all to families. His personal life has leaned more toward drama than comedy. He has battled alcoholism, spent time in jail for drug dealing, and seen his marriage deteriorate.

Allen faced difficult times in his childhood as well. His real name is Timothy Allen Dick, and as a child he was teased about his name. His father died when he was eleven, and his family moved more than a thousand miles from Denver to Detroit after his mother remarried. Rebellion and apathy, sprinkled with his witty remarks and comebacks, marked his high school and college years, and he hit a low point after being arrested for dealing drugs.

Allen hasn't let difficult times or his mistakes keep him down. After spending time in prison, he focused on his career, turning his stand-up act into a successful television show and acting career. At one point, he had the number-one television show, the top movie, and a book leading the best-seller list. After succeeding with comedies, Allen is interested in taking his acting still further with more dramatic roles.

Despite all his success, at heart Allen still thinks of himself as a guy who loves tinkering with cars and puttering around the house, someone grounded in Midwestern loyalties and sensibilities. As

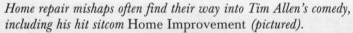

Home repair mishaps often find their way into Tim Allen's comedy, including his hit sitcom Home Improvement *(pictured).*

Tim Dick, he used humor to fend off jokes about his name, gain friends in school, and make it through a prison sentence. As Tim Allen, he kept his down-to-earth attitude and polished the sharp wit that got him through those tough times, using it to do what he loves best: make audiences laugh.

Success has not made life easier for Allen. Hard work boosted his career, but time away from his family eroded his relationship with his wife. Allen has been on top in several facets of the entertainment industry, but instead of making him content it has left him looking for other ways to measure his worth. He has a philosophical bent, a thoughtful side that is much deeper than his one-dimensional television character would indicate. At times, Allen wishes he could view life through the simple eyes of the characters he has created. Then he could be certain that the choices he is making are the ones that will lead to a fulfilling life. But real life is never that easy.

Much of Tim Allen's success has to do with his competitive nature and a quest to conquer the next challenge that comes his way. It drives him to continue to look for new dimensions to add to his career, even though part of him wonders what the cost will be to his personal life. He's realistic enough to know that not every move he makes will be a resounding success, but he's competitive enough to keep trying.

Chapter 1

Starts and Stops

Timothy Allen Dick was born on June 13, 1953, in Denver, Colorado. When he entered show business years later, Tim shortened his name to Tim Allen. But as a child he was known as Tim Dick, son of Gerald and Martha Dick. He was the third of five boys and a girl who lived in a nice house on Marion Street, right down the road from the country club. Tim's dad was a successful businessman, working in insurance and real estate. His mom kept things running smoothly at home.

There was always something going on at the Dick household. With half a dozen children in the family and friends who often stopped by, there was ample opportunity for Tim to play games and get into mischief. The Dicks lived comfortably, and young Tim had few worries. As a youngster, his world revolved around his family, his friends, and his bike. He hung out with a gang of friends, riding his bike, eating junk food, and looking for something exciting to do. "Little boys are animals," he wrote in the autobiographical *Don't Stand Too Close to a Naked Man*. "They're indestructible creatures made of sticks and stones and ball bearings. Their mission is clear: push the boundaries wherever possible."[3]

Tim and his brothers spent their days playing games and thriving on adrenaline-pumping pastimes. When it was time to eat, they didn't exactly worry about their table manners. To emphasize their hunger, they acted like animals, emitting grunting sounds while waiting for supper. Tim later used this sound as part of his comedy act.

One of Tim's favorite games as a child was playing war. Tim, his brothers, and friends invented elaborate war games, hiding behind bushes and firing toy guns. When a neighbor built his version of a pillbox, a fort for a machine gun, Tim loaded a toy bazooka with a sparkler, shot it, and set the pillbox on fire. Fortunately, no one was injured, and for Tim and his friends, the thrill of his conquest outweighed any danger involved with his methods.

When games of war got boring, Tim turned his attention to BB guns. He tried shooting at animals, but after he shot a squirrel and a bird, the realization hit him that he had ended their lives. From then on, he shot at nonliving targets instead.

Tim couldn't subdue his penchant for making trouble, however. Although he shot at a number of tin cans, he also shot at traffic lights and a neighbor's windows, and found it exciting to destroy other things as well. Tim and his brothers would build model airplanes just so they could set them on fire in mock battles. These games were dangerous, and one of his friends endured a painful injury when hot plastic fell on his hand.

Like these boys, Allen spent many hours playing war as a child.

In addition to his dangerous pursuits, Tim also had his share of innocent childhood fun. He went to summer camp, had a newspaper route, and cooled off on hot summer days with a swim at the local pool. He and his friends burned off energy by playing kick-the-can and other neighborhood games.

Not every childhood moment was exciting and fun for Tim, however. Other children found humor in his last name and enjoyed teasing him about it. After a while, Tim knew the jokes would be coming whenever he met someone new, so he learned to defend himself with humor. He developed a series of quick retorts he could use to defuse the situation and make those who taunted him the subject of the joke instead. He also made his friends laugh by speaking in unusual voices or making animal sounds. Although he sometimes went too far, occasionally hurting others' feelings or irritating them with annoying noises, he was already showing signs of the wit and comic timing that would serve him well as an adult.

An Understanding Dad

Tim got his sense of humor and quick wit from his dad. Gerald Dick added zest to any gathering he attended. He had a knack for making people laugh, a trait Tim shared.

Gerald Dick had an easygoing nature and used instruction rather than punishment to try to keep Tim and his brothers safe when they got into risky territory. When a firecracker blew off Tim's thumbnail, for example, his father didn't get upset. He simply told him that he had held the firecracker too long. As an adult, Tim recalled that his dad once showed him how to make a mortar, a device used to fire things high into the air. "From my adult perspective this seems like both a good and bad thing," Allen said. "Dads are not supposed to teach their kids to be terrorists, but I guess he knew we'd try it on our own, so he figured we might as well learn to do it the right way."[4]

Gerald Dick also taught Tim about two more things that would become important in his life: tools and cars. Gerald was always tinkering with the family car, putting on a dual exhaust or making the family station wagon faster and louder. Tim enjoyed working on the car with his dad, and going to drag races with his dad and brothers. Another of their favorite activities was visiting the hardware section of the Sears store near their home.

Tragedy

Tim grew up with a strong circle of friends to play with and a supportive family at home. However, his comfortable childhood was disrupted on a Saturday in November 1964. While Tim stayed home to play with a friend, his father drove his wife, two of his sons, and some of their friends to a University of Colorado football game in Boulder. On the way home from the game, a driver who had been drinking hit the car Tim's dad was driving. Gerald Dick managed to maneuver the car out of the way the best he could, but couldn't avoid a collision. He was the only one killed in the accident.

It was difficult for Tim to accept the loss of his father. One minute he was living a carefree childhood; the next, his father was gone. Tim's brothers, sister, and mother leaned on each other after the tragedy. They all felt the anguish of the loss of Gerald Dick and consoled each other. "Everyone pulled together to help each other out," Allen said. "We had a 'support system' without knowing what the heck one was."[5]

Despite the support he got from his family, Tim was overwhelmed by the enormity and suddenness of the loss and found it difficult to adjust to life without his dad. Although he knew he had nothing to do with the accident, he couldn't help wondering if he could have done something to prevent it. If he had done anything different earlier in the day, would the collision have been avoided? "At eleven years old . . . you don't understand why your father was there one minute and ripped away from you the next," he said. "It blindsided me and I don't like being blindsided by people."[6]

Tim was angry, and realized how little control he had over events that impacted his life. He even felt resentment for the carefree happiness that had marked his life before the accident, because having it taken away made him feel the pain that much more deeply. He felt like he had been awakened too early from a delightful dream, and realized that the world made no promises that tomorrow bring happiness.

Allen learned about cars from his father. The comedian is pictured with his treasured Ford "32 Deuce" hot rod.

New Beginning

Tim's mother did the best she could to hold her family together in the aftermath of her husband's death. For support, she turned to her own family in Michigan. She found solace in those visits, and on one of the trips home was reacquainted with a high school sweetheart.

Their old friendship blossomed into love, and in 1966 Tim's mother married William Bones. When Tim was thirteen, his family moved from Denver to Michigan. They lived in affluent Birmingham, a suburb of Detroit, and Tim became part of a blended family, with two new brothers and a new sister. It wasn't easy for Tim to leave his friends behind in Colorado, but he didn't have a choice. His stepdad had a job in Michigan, so that was where the family had to live. Tim eventually grew close to his new dad and siblings and saw how his mother's marriage to Bones

Tim and His Siblings

Tim Allen grew up in a large blended family, with seven boys and two girls. In a family that large, there are bound to be some scuffles between the siblings. Tim's family was no exception. He had two older brothers who liked to pick on him when his parents weren't around, until Tim decided he had had enough. "I finally hit the ringleader brother one day," Tim recalled in an interview with a *Calgary Sun* reporter. "He plowed me good, but we had a truce after that."

Tim was far from a saint, however, in his own role as big brother. Instead of bullying his younger brother, he tormented him with underhandedness. "I'd cheat when we played games," Tim remembered years later. "I'd always make him lose and it frustrated him so very much. He never caught on. What I did weighed on my conscience. I've apologized to him since."

helped both families. Years later he wrote of his stepfamily, "Their love rescued us all."[7]

Fast Cars

Tim came to love and respect his stepfather, even dedicating his first book to him. He wrote, he "stepped up to the plate and hit a home run for all of us."[8] However, as a rebellious teen, Tim did not always listen to his new father. He wasn't interested in bonding with his mother's new husband, who did not share Tim's passion for things like cars. Tim wanted to do things with his friends and insisted on going to drag races on Woodward Avenue, which led from the center of Detroit to its suburbs. The races were fast and dangerous.

Since they had nine children to feed and clothe, Tim's family wasn't wealthy enough for him to afford his own hot rod. However, he hung around with guys whose parents worked for one of the big Detroit automakers, so they had their own fast cars. With his love of cars, Tim was a welcome addition to the crowd watching the races. The roar of the engines, the speed of the race, and the thrill of doing something that was forbidden were all enticing to him.

Tim was part of a popular group of students at Seaholm High School. On Saturday mornings he could often be found hanging around at a friend's house playing foosball, a table game in which player figures attached to rods are moved to kick a small ball up and down the table. Tim wasn't an outstanding student at Seaholm. He was popular, smart, and funny, but he drifted through school rather than bothering to put his energy into his studies. Always good with his hands, he enjoyed shop class but didn't like the teachers. "If there was no opportunity for me to be a smart ass, then I wouldn't be happy,"[9] he said. Because of his interest in cars, he thought he might work in the auto industry or drive a truck after high school, but he had no concrete plans for the rest of his life.

Tim's innate talent for comedy was already apparent, however. He mentioned to a classmate that one day he would be on *The Tonight Show* with Johnny Carson, a milestone for comedians. During graduation week, he served as the master of ceremonies for Swingout, the school's talent show. Although he felt comfortable in front of an audience, he lacked the focus to direct himself toward a career in comedy at this stage in his life.

College

After graduating from Seaholm in 1971, Allen attended Central Michigan University in Mount Pleasant. Several of his high school friends attended the school as well, and Allen found plenty of time to party with his friends between his television production classes. After two years at Central, Allen transferred to Western Michigan

Allen, pictured here as a senior at Seaholm High School, was popular because of his quick wit but he channeled little of his energy into schoolwork.

Detroit

As a child, Tim Allen lived in Denver, Colorado, and then near Detroit, Michigan, two cities with very different personalities. Detroit, an industrial center in the Midwest, is known for making automobiles and Motown music. In fact, Detroit had produced more automobiles and trucks than any other city in the world. Called the Motor City, it is on the southeastern border of the state, across the Detroit River from Canada. When he was in high school, Allen had many friends whose fathers worked in the automotive industry, and Allen found many buddies who were as passionate about cars as he was.

Despite its problems with crime and overcrowded schools, Allen loved Detroit and the state of Michigan. He chose Detroit as the setting for his television show and included Detroit Lions T-shirts in his character Tim Taylor's wardrobe. A summer vacation episode of *Home Improvement* was filmed near Traverse City, Michigan, and Allen's character made frequent references to his hometown. "I didn't want the show set in New York or California," Allen told the *Detroit Free Press*. "I wanted it in Detroit because I'm from there, but also there's something about the Midwest. It's more comfortable, more down-to-earth. It's a place where you *really* appreciate any good weather you get for time out on your patio."

Allen was happy to return to Detroit in the summer of 2001 for the Detroit 300 Celebrity Homecoming, as well as his thirtieth class reunion at Seaholm High School. "I am such a Detroit fan," said Allen, who owns a home in the Detroit area and a cottage in Omena Point. "It was always a cool city. I've always loved it, mostly because it's an underdog. And I've always rooted for underdogs."

University in Kalamazoo. There, he studied both philosophy and television production, fueling his interests in introspection and entertainment.

While working toward his degree in television production, Allen was part of a zany radio comedy show called *The Five Finger Salute*. He and the other members of the cast put together thirty minutes of off-the-wall skits each week, trying on different characters and putting out oddball comedy. The show and accolades from his professors proved that Allen had the talent to pursue a career in comedy, but he was still unsure of what to do with his life after graduating from college in 1976.

Arresting Situation

While in college, Allen had fallen in with a party crowd. He used and sold drugs. At times he talked about making just one more deal and getting out, but he sunk deeper and deeper into the abyss of drug dealing. He couldn't resist the seemingly easy money he made dealing drugs, and while he was making money this way, he couldn't see any reason to pursue a regular job. But he also couldn't shake the feeling that, as he got more involved in selling drugs, the way out would be more difficult. "I didn't have any idea what I was going to do with my life, and the money was right," he said. "I was floundering, actually. That's how I got into trouble. By 1978 I was getting very worried about where I was going."[10]

Allen set up his last drug deal in 1978. He and a partner agreed to meet a buyer at the Kalamazoo Airport. Allen suspected that the man was a cop but figured it was worth taking a chance. He thought he would be able to escape into the airport if the deal was a setup. Allen's plan didn't work, however. He was right, the buyer was a cop, and Allen was arrested for selling $42,000 of cocaine to an undercover police officer. "Doing it was dumb," he said years later. "I was asking to get caught, I think. Why did I do it? I don't know, it seemed a quick, exciting way to get easy money."[11]

Sobering Events

Allen had stumbled through high school and college right into a nightmare. As a student, he had shown he had a knack for making people laugh, but rather than sharpen that part of his personality, he chose to pursue a lifestyle that offered danger and quick cash. The danger and boyish mischief of childhood and the drag races of his teen years that had sent his adrenaline rushing had been replaced by a life-threatening lifestyle, resulting in an encounter with the law. It was a sobering experience for Allen, who hadn't really considered the consequences of his actions. He had gotten into drug dealing so deeply, however, that an arrest was the safest way out. Years later, he saw his arrest as a positive turning point in his life. "I'm kinda fortunate it came apart, because I think with a little more practice, I would have gotten really good at it,"[12] he said.

After his comfortable childhood had been disrupted by the death of his father, Allen had seemed to adjust to his mother's remarriage and his family's move to Michigan. However, he never focused on his future, and didn't make plans that would put his talents to their best use. His bad decisions cost him dearly, as his trouble with the law took him down a difficult path.

Chapter 2

Revving Up

ALLEN HAD COME face-to-face with the consequences of his drug dealing. After reveling in the freedom of college and enjoying a postcollege lifestyle marked by irresponsibility, Allen's life changed abruptly. He could not do as he pleased. He was no longer a free man.

After his arrest, Allen spent sixty days in a holding cell with nine other inmates. His sparse accommodations had metal benches along the wall and a toilet in the middle. He said his dismal surroundings were like a "cauldron of despair." [13] He had come from the suburbs, from a comfortable family life. Now he was surrounded by criminals who had survived much tougher upbringings, and he was terrified of how he would be treated.

In the holding cell, Allen was stripped of his privacy. He was so frightened that he hesitated to use the toilet in the center of the cell. When he could stand it no longer and sat down to use the toilet, the other prisoners moved toward him. To his relief, they formed a semicircle around him to give him privacy.

When Allen called his parents and told them where he was, they were shocked and disappointed. However, while he was in jail, their first priority was to help him get out. They didn't ask why or how he had fallen into drug dealing, at least not right away. First they wanted to help him out of the mess he had made of his life.

Allen gradually came to fully understand how serious his situation was. He had flirted with danger, as he so often had when he was a child. But this time he did more than injure a thumbnail. He now faced the possibility of spending the rest of his life in prison. Shortly before his arrest, Michigan had passed tough antidrug legislation that called for anyone selling more than a pound of cocaine, as Allen had done, to spend life in prison without parole. At twenty-five years old, Allen could have seen the last of the outside world.

After spending two months in the holding cell, Allen stayed with his parents in Bloomfield Hills while waiting to be sentenced. This time he listened to what they had to say and obeyed their rules. He also took the advice of his lawyer, who suggested he plead guilty. To increase his chances of a lighter sentence, Allen made a deal with the police. He helped them arrest twenty-one other people involved in drug dealing. As a result of the deal, one serious charge was dropped, and it was agreed that Allen would be sentenced in federal court, which meant that he would not have to be sentenced under Michigan's tough anticrime law. "I knew what I did was wrong," Allen told reporter Daniel Cerone in the *Los Angeles Times*. "I did not drag it out in a trial. I knew I made a major mistake." [14]

A young man languishes in jail. Allen also spent time in jail after his arrest for drug dealing.

Comedy

For the time being, Allen was able to stay out of jail. He had nine months to wait before he was sentenced for his crime. His lawyer advised him to stay busy in order to keep his mind off the day when a judge in a courtroom would decide his fate.

After years of drifting through life without a concrete plan for where he wanted to go, Allen now needed to focus on a clear goal. He had to make the best possible use of his time and build a solid reputation before his sentencing. If he proved that he was now a responsible citizen, there was a chance the judge would give him a lighter sentence or no jail time at all. To prove that he could hold down a job, Allen took a position as a salesman at a sporting goods store.

While working at the store, Allen encountered a comedian named Eric Head, who was trying to make it as a stand-up comic in the Detroit area. Impressed by Allen's witty rapport with customers, Head suggested that Allen try performing at Mark Ridley's Room of Comedy and Magic, later renamed the Comedy Castle, in Detroit. Allen was hesitant to go onstage right away, but he went with Head and other friends to see a few acts. While watching the other comedians perform, Allen's confidence in his own ability as a comedian grew. He wrote a series of jokes and accepted a dare from his friend Bill Ludwig to go onstage with his act.

In February 1979, Allen was set to make his debut. However, the usually self-assured Allen came down with a severe case of opening night jitters. Before going onstage, Allen paced nervously. His hands shook. Ludwig tried to reassure his friend; he knew he had the talent to make it.

Once he was onstage, Allen realized that he did, too. He was in control. The laughs came slowly at first but built to a steady flow as he became more confident. The audience loved him. Allen was a hit and now knew what he wanted to do with his life. "I was always making wisecracks; the world seemed upside down and kind of crazy to me then—it still does—so I figured, 'Why not put the two together?'" Allen said. "At first I was just trying to keep my own spirits up, but then I found out I could make other people laugh, and I thought, 'Hey—this is cool. I like this.'" [15] Soon after, Allen saw

Laughs in the Motor City

Tim Allen began his stand-up comedy career at a time when Detroit was on the cusp of becoming one of the hottest towns for comedy in the country. In January 1979, Mark Ridley opened Mark Ridley's Room of Comedy and Magic, based on comedy clubs he'd visited in Los Angeles. It would become one of the premier clubs in the Midwest, but before Ridley could draw the big-name talent he had seen on the West Coast, he needed to establish the club with solid local acts.

At twenty-five, Allen delivered his first stand-up routine at Ridley's establishment, which had been renamed the Comedy Castle. Before having to leave the club to serve his jail sentence, Allen was the club's headliner. The city's comedy scene continued to grow while he was in jail. More comedy clubs opened in the city and the Comedy Castle began to attract national headliners, such as Jerry Seinfeld, Jay Leno, and Dennis Miller. Fellow Detroit comedian Dave Coulier went to Los Angeles and was cast on the series *Full House.*

After serving his time in prison, Allen eased back into the comedy scene at the Comedy Castle. He opened for the headliners while polishing his material, and eventually moved on to clubs around the country at a time when stand-up comedy was hot. The comedy boom sagged in Detroit and around the nation in the 1990s, as clubs closed and audiences watched their favorite comedians on television. However, the stand-up comedy scene rebounded in the Motor City early this century as Detroit boasted ten clubs dedicated to comedy and a host of other venues offering stand-up a few nights a week.

Allen performs at a festival celebrating Detroit's 300th birthday in 2001.

a concert film by comedian Richard Pryor, and the audience's re-
sponse to Pryor's jokes made Allen even more determined to become a professional comedian. He wanted to be the person who
could wash away someone's bad day with well-timed humor.

Allen began performing regularly at the Comedy Castle.
Dressed in a suit and tie, he presented a professional image that set
him apart from other performers. He got along well with the circle
of comics who performed at the club and was loved by the audience. Before long, he was the club's top act. However, just when
he finally found his calling, he had another engagement waiting for
him that he couldn't get out of. "I'd done well enough to become
the number one boy before I had to tell [the manager], 'Hey, I'm
going to have to take a little time off. Let me try to explain,'" [16]
Allen said.

Prison

In November 1979, Allen was sentenced to eight years in a federal
penitentiary. He had used his time before his sentencing wisely,
and his hard work was taken into account. However, he still had
to pay for the crime he had committed. At his sentencing,
Kalamazoo County circuit judge Patrick McCauley noted Allen's
potential for making others laugh. "There is a remarkable talent–
don't waste it," McCauley told Allen. "Be a man. Do your time.
Then come out and do what you do best. I expect you to be a very
successful comedian." [17]

Allen was sent to Sandstone Federal Correctional Institution in
Sandstone, Minnesota. The prison was a frightening and dreary
place, but even in those surroundings Allen maintained a sense of
humor. He had to in order to get through the long days and to get
along with his fellow prisoners.

Accepting Responsibility

Even though he was able to make jokes while behind bars, Allen
still hated the fact that he was in prison. But instead of being angry
at the people and circumstances that had put him there, he was angry with himself for getting into that situation. He eventually realized that anger wouldn't make his sentence any shorter, and dealt
with life in his new surroundings by making plans for the future.

Demonstrating the promise noted by the judge who had sentenced him to prison, Allen has become a highly successful actor and comic.

He vowed never to get involved with drugs again and worked on his comedy act while he was behind bars. Admitting his guilt and planning for the future helped Allen put his life of drug dealing behind him for good. "It helped to say I committed the offense," he said. "It allowed me to tear my house down, if you will, and build from scratch. I made a conscious effort to stay busy and not become the angry young man, while all around me there were these guys saying, 'I didn't do it.'" [18]

Allen's family supported him and helped him get through these difficult times. They could see he was sorry for what he had done and wanted to change his life. "Tim accepted it," his mother

Humor Behind Bars

Prison is not a place that lends itself to humor. However, Allen found that if he could inject a little levity into the lives of other prisoners, they wouldn't beat him up. Laughs inside prison were rare, and as long as Allen could get his fellow prisoners to chuckle, he was safe. "Humor was the only defense I had," he told reporter Susan Schindehette in *People Weekly*. "Two minutes after I was there, I started babbling. So everyone knew I was a geek right away."

One prisoner cracked up every time Allen imitated Elmer Fudd. The guards laughed when Allen put a picture of President Richard Nixon in the peephole of his cell. Allen even did his stand-up routine for the other inmates. One time, however, Allen's jokes went too far.

The prison had a toastmaster's club so that the prisoners could work on their speaking skills. Allen became president of the club and gave a speech needling the outgoing president. His jokes were too critical for the other prisoner's taste, however, and the other prisoner threatened to beat Allen up. However, as the prisoner was holding Allen against the wall, something about the situation made Allen think of a goofy look his brother used to make. Allen started laughing. The other prisoner didn't know what to make of Allen's odd behavior and let him go.

said. "He knew he deserved it, and he didn't fight it. Everyone in the family came out and rallied behind him."[19] He also got support from his girlfriend, Laura Deibel, whom he had met while he was in college. She would visit the comedy club while Allen was in prison, making mental notes so she could give him updates on the material that the other comedians were using and tell him how they fared in front of an audience.

Allen stayed in touch with his old friends by writing letters. He corresponded with Ridley so he wouldn't be forgotten at the Comedy Castle. Allen wanted to be sure there would be a place for him onstage after he had served his time.

Allen realized he had hit bottom but could use this time to turn his life around. If he hadn't been caught, he would have probably continued to deal drugs and might have been killed. Spending time in prison was not pleasant, but it gave him the chance to rebuild his life. He could start over with the knowledge that he had changed and overcome the challenges of life behind bars. After spending more than a year in a federal prison, Allen was paroled. He was determined to make something of his life.

"In retrospect, I realize [those years] taught me that life often takes you to new and often unexpected areas, and these can cause a lot of conflict and challenge," he said. "But I learned that however these affect you, you can't run from them: Problems have legs, too, and they have a habit of running in the same direction as you."[20]

Back to Work

Allen lived in a halfway house for several months after being released from prison. At the halfway house were other former inmates who were readjusting to life outside prison. Allen returned to his job at the sporting goods store but had to be back to the halfway house by a certain time each night or he could go back to jail. After his time at the halfway house was over, he had more freedom in his choice of living quarters but still had to periodically check in with a parole officer for several years.

In addition to his job at the sporting goods store, Allen also did some script writing for an agency owned by some of his friends from high school. He also did some work in television commercials, thanks to his friend Eric Head. Head worked at a large advertising agency and helped Allen land roles in commercials for Big Boy restaurants, Pella Windows, and Tuffy Mufflers. Allen also appeared in television ads for Ford, Chevrolet, Kmart, and Mr. Goodwrench.

Allen didn't forget his comedy career, however. He went back to the Comedy Castle and impressed his fellow comedians with his act, which didn't appear to have suffered from the time Allen spent in prison. Allen was eventually able to leave his other jobs to focus solely on his career in comedy.

Touring

Even though Allen was a modest success, he sought to improve his act. The best way for him to improve his act was to get up in front of an audience, which he did every chance he got. He appeared at comedy clubs around the United States. He played bars, clubs, conventions, and even a library. He was intent on getting as much time onstage and as much exposure in as many venues as possible.

He videotaped his performances so he could rewatch them and work on his routine.

Allen's most loyal fan during the early years of his career was his girlfriend, Laura. Allen was amazed that she stayed with him through it all, but she said it was a simple decision because they loved each other. During the day, Laura was a sales manager for an interior landscaper. In the evening, she would try to be in the audience when Allen performed. She would sit in the back of the room, ready to greet him with a big hug and kiss when he was finished with his routine. Allen was awed by her support, and their love and commitment to each other continued to grow. Allen and Laura were married on April 7, 1984.

Intent on improving his comedy act, Allen appeared at comedy clubs like this one throughout the country.

Allen's wife Laura supported his comedy career, but his scatological humor and stories about his jail time often left audiences cold.

Powering Up

Laura gave her husband support and encouragement, but there was still something lacking in Allen's comedy routine. His material included jokes about his experiences in jail as well as many references to sex and bathroom humor. However, audiences couldn't connect with his stories about jail, and his routine sometimes fell flat. Allen had to find something audiences could relate to. One night in 1984, in front of a group of Goodyear tire salesmen in Akron, Ohio, he found it.

Allen was telling prison jokes and floundering. He needed to do something, and it all came together once he realized how simple a man's sense of humor can be. Allen just started naming power tools. He immediately connected with his audience as he made fun of men and the tools they love. He got laughs out of variable-speed routers, super-powered sanders, and plumb lines. He made jokes about garages, hubcaps, and tractors. "As I was dying up there, I was thinking, Tim—what you need is something these guys can relate to, and I thought . . . tires . . . cars . . . tools. I love cars, and I figured these guys must love them, too," he said. "So I just started naming tools, and as I did that, I growled like my brothers and I used to do when we sat around the dinner table waiting to eat." [21]

Allen soon broadened his act to include jokes about things men do differently than women. He noted that, when watching television, women look to connect with the relationships and the story. Men are looking for the instant thrills of explosions, car chases, and fires. He also bragged that he had such a powerful lawn mower that his wife had to act as his pit crew. His fans cheered him on and grunted along with him. As he brought his act to audiences around the country, some even started wearing pig masks to his shows, in reference to his tag line "Men are pigs." "What really interested me was garages and tools and all that I call 'men's stuff,'" Allen said. "The more I started talking about it, the more I would get men to stand up and listen to my comedy. And then women would go, '[My husband's] like that,' and it started getting couples to enjoy the show." [22]

Television

As Allen's popularity grew, his manager, Elaine Steffek, got him booked at the top comedy clubs on the West Coast, such as the Ice House in Pasadena, California. Television executives and producers often visited the Ice House, and this gave Allen the exposure he needed to get national television appearances. In 1988 he appeared in *Comedy's Dirtiest Dozen* and the *Showtime Comedy Club*

All-Stars II. In 1989 he was part of *The Five O'Clock Funnies* on radio station KLOS in Los Angeles. The station aired clips from his
stand-up act and increased his fan base. That year he was also on
the television special *Opening Night at Rodney's Place.*

Allen's popularity continued to build, and in 1989 he hired
two managers with a background in the entertainment business.
Richard Baker and Rick Messina helped Allen get his own television special on Showtime. In 1990 Allen taped *Tim Allen: Men Are
Pigs.* In a routine liberally laced with profanity and vulgar comments, Allen poked fun at his grandmother, housework, lawn care,
women, makeup, tool belts, and visits to the hardware store. His
routine was punctuated with grunts and ape noises. The audience
loved him, and his popularity was evident. The special was filmed
in Kalamazoo, Michigan, where Allen was well known, and his
Midwestern fans enthusiastically applauded his performance.

Big Break

Later that year, Allen, who had been
nominated for Male Stand-Up
Comic of the Year, came to the attention of a group of Disney executives
who were looking for new talent.
They were watching videos of
promising acts, but what they saw
practically put them to sleep. Then
they came across a video of Allen's
stand-up act. "He set the room on
fire," said Jeffrey Katzenberg, who
was the head of Disney movies. "It
was like everyone had touched a raw
electric wire."[23] Disney chief Michael
Eisner then went to see Allen perform at the Improv in Los Angeles
and was so impressed that he offered

*Disney head Michael Eisner (pictured) was
so struck by Allen's talent that he offered to
develop a television show for him.*

to put him in a television series. "It was one of those nights that was magic," Allen said. "They came backstage and said they'd like to have a meeting with me at Disney."[24]

Allen was scared and nervous about acting, but he believed that he could do the funny stuff that came naturally to him, such as make an expression or use a gesture to get a laugh. He agreed to do a pilot for Disney but was choosy about what the pilot would be. Though he was flattered to have been chosen by Disney, he had seen other stand-up comics have short-lived television shows. He did not want to be a fresh new face for a doomed project. After all, he had a thriving stand-up career and didn't want to jeopardize everything he had worked for.

Doing what was best for his daughter, Kate, who was born in 1990, also entered in to his decision. Accepting the challenge of a television series meant the family would likely have to relocate from Michigan to California. It would also mean they would need to adjust to a more demanding schedule for Allen. As a stand-up comic, Allen had done his share of traveling but was able to spend time at home between weekend engagements. A series would put more demands on his time during the week. It would be a boon to the family financially and would be a great career move for Allen, but there would be a cost to his personal life.

The Right Move

Allen decided to see what type of television series Disney could offer him. He was first offered a sitcom based on the movie *Turner and Hooch,* which had starred Tom Hanks, and another based on the movie *Dead Poets Society,* which had starred Robin Williams. Allen hesitated to take over characters that had already been established by other actors. He turned these series down because he didn't want to do something that wasn't right for him just for the money.

Instead, Allen offered his own idea. He thought a series based on his stand-up act, centered around a handyman who loved power tools, would be the best way for him to bring his talent as a comedian into a television series. He was making a bold career decision and wanted to do it with a character he was comfortable with. "This was a big move," he said, "and I don't mean just the money, but the commitment. I'd been doing standup for all these

Allen proposed that his sitcom character, pictured in this scene from Home Improvement, *capitalize on his stand-up routines about home repair and power tools.*

years, and finally reached the stage where I could work on weekends and spend the rest of the time with my wife and daughter. But I loved that character, and I wanted to see what it would be like to put him in a family situation. I did the pilot episode [for *Home Improvement*], not really sure I wanted this kind of life. Then the series sold, and it was too late."[25]

While the production of *Home Improvement* was under discussion, Allen continued his stand-up career. In 1990 he hosted the *Just for Laughs International Comedy Festival* in Montreal, Canada. The special was taped and shown on cable television. Allen's hosting job earned him a Cable ACE Award for best performance in a comedy special. He beat out notable comedian Billy Crystal, who had been nominated for an HBO special. So little was known about Allen in Hollywood that his win had HBO president Michael Fuchs fuming, and wondering who Allen was. Before long, however, there would be little chance that any entertainment executive in America wouldn't recognize Allen's name.

Putting His Foot Down

Allen had gone through some difficult times, but his arrest and uncertainty over his future freedom made him finally make plans for his life. He accepted the challenge of putting his wisecracks and witty rapport into an act and opening himself up onstage. Allen was determined to succeed at comedy, and once he had that goal in mind, he didn't waver. He spent years polishing his act in clubs around the country, gaining more and more recognition until he finally came to the attention of people who could make him a household name all over America.

Allen had done a remarkable job of controlling his career and guiding himself to this level of success. Now his challenge would be to keep his career on an upward swing without losing control of the character he had created, and maintain a stable family life. He had been on the comedy circuit long enough to know the demands that came with a performing career and was afraid that more career opportunities would jeopardize his family life. However, he also wanted to see how far he could take his talent, and couldn't pass up a chance to reach for a bigger prize.

Chapter 3

Cruising

ALLEN WAS EXCITED and nervous about the direction his career was heading. He had labored on the comedy circuit for almost a decade, and his hard work was paying off with a starring role in a television series. But he had pressured the studio to let him have a show based on a character he had created. If it failed, he would be held accountable. Allen was confident in his ability to do stand-up comedy but wasn't certain he could transfer those skills to a weekly television show. He had the potential to take his career to a new level of success, and now had to deal with the pressure to live up to that potential.

Before Allen worried too much about his career, however, he celebrated in his own way. In typical macho style, he bought an $800 compost shredder for his home in Beverly Hills, Michigan. A reporter asked him if he got anything for his wife. His face serious, he replied, "Oh, sure. I bought her a lawnmower."[26]

Before taping for *Home Improvement* began, Allen took steps to give it a better chance of being a success. He showed he was serious about his new job by enrolling in acting classes at the University of Detroit. He had been in front of the camera before, for his college classes and his comedy specials, but he knew that doing a television series would be different than a class project or simply having his stand-up act taped. He would have to learn to interact with other actors, not the audience, and show a wider range of emotions than his stand-up act required.

In the series he would also have to modify the stand-up character he had created. While he maintained the essence of a man who loved tools and cars and was perplexed by women, the rough, vulgar language of his stand-up act was not suitable for a prime-time audience. Allen wouldn't be able to punctuate his punch lines with swear words in order to get a laugh. He knew he had work to do. "Before *Home Improvement,* the sum total of my acting experience was appearing in the background of a Mr. Goodwrench commercial," Allen admitted. "On the other hand, the funny stuff comes very naturally to me, so I can do things–like a gesture or an expression–that the others might not think of to get a laugh."[27]

While he worked to make his show a success, a part of Allen found it hard to believe he had been given this opportunity. He didn't feel like a rising Hollywood star. He felt more like a Michigan comedian polishing his next gig. In fact, Allen didn't dramatically change his lifestyle once he signed the contract for his series. He kept his home in Michigan and his Midwestern sensibilities. "He just never lost perspective," said Bruce Economou, a friend from Michigan. "When he first went to the *Home Improvement* stage, where they were building the sets, and the people from Disney were walking him through, they told him, 'This is all for you.' Tim looked at it and said, 'Well, if this show doesn't work, can I have the wood?'"[28]

Problems from the Past

Allen was hesitant to embrace his new status as an actor, and his reaction was nearly prophetic. *Home Improvement* was almost doomed before it had a chance to air. During the past few years, Allen had successfully kept his prison time quiet as he promoted himself on the comedy circuit. When interviewed by reporters, he steered away from questions that touched on his past, concentrating instead on his act and where his career was going. However, as his career blossomed, his past was sure to become a very public subject.

As production on *Home Improvement* began, there were rumors about Allen's prison record and past drug use. His past wasn't something that would be easy to keep secret forever, because many people Allen had worked with in the Detroit area knew he had spent time in prison. But Allen saw no need to discuss a time in his life that was over and done with. He didn't feel his past had any relevance to the present. He had paid his dues and then moved on with his life. However, as he became a bigger star, the public began to want to know more about him. Sensational stories about his past were bound to appear. Allen had to decide whether to try to minimize his

Home Improvement

In *Home Improvement,* Tim Allen plays Tim "the Toolman" Taylor, the Detroit handyman host of *Tool Time,* a cable television show. Like Allen's stand-up character, the television Tim is addicted to power—as in power tools. He believes he can supercharge his lawn mower and his family's household appliances.

Balancing Tim's preoccupation with power are his levelheaded wife (played by Patricia Richardson) and three sons (played by Zachery Ty Bryan, Jonathan Taylor Thomas, and Taran Noah Smith). They are well aware of the limitations of Tim's abilities, but also know that he's always trying to do the right thing for his family. It's not Tim's ability with a hammer but his ability to grow a little in each episode while maintaining his overtly masculine touch that endeared him to his on-screen family and his legions of fans.

The undercurrent of family support in the show is strengthened by Wilson, the family's neighbor, who dispenses philosophical advice over the fence between the families' two yards. *People Weekly* noted that Wilson added wisdom to the show, telling Tim things like, "Men need to spend more time around the campfire with their elders like in the ancient days, seeking wisdom, telling stories, sharing." Wilson is seen only from the eyes up, partly to give him a mystical aura but also as a gimmick to make the show memorable.

The show had other touches that set it apart from other series as well. Computer animation enhanced the ending of a scene, with effects such as having the final image break apart like glass. The show also ended with outtakes from the filming, showing Allen's spontaneity as well as the general upbeat mood on the set. The combination of family values, humor, and special touches kept the series hot for its eight-year run.

Allen as Tim Taylor is pictured here with television neighbor Wilson.

past and cover up what he could or confess that he had once spent time in prison and had had a drug problem. Either way, he risked the loss of his prized television series.

Faced with the dilemma of whether to open up about his past, Allen and his wife discussed the situation. He also sought advice from an old friend and consulted a public relations firm. With their guidance, he came to the conclusion that it was best to tell the truth. The facts about his time in prison would probably come to light whether he tried to cover them up or not, and it would look much worse for him if the media uncovered his mistakes. If he admitted to them up front, he would be in control of how the news was delivered.

Exposing his past was not an easy decision for Allen. But when Matt Williams, the executive producer of *Home Improvement*, called Allen looking for a straight story after hearing rumors of his drug use, Allen told him the truth. Williams urged Allen to allow the story to be told to the public. "When I told him we ought to release the story, in a straightforward and thoughtful manner, his knee-jerk reaction was, yes, we should tell the truth, but he didn't want his family dragged through the mud and hurt," Williams said. "I told him that, if he wanted to protect his family, and minimize [adverse publicity], his best course of action was to be straight. Candor, honesty—those things are appreciated by everybody."[29]

Waiting and Wondering

In mid-August, Allen told ABC executives and Disney about his past drug use and prison record for drug dealing. They stood by him and the show. Then he told the national press and waited for reaction from fans. "It was an extremely intense couple of weeks," his wife said. "If we were Three Mile Island, we would have had a meltdown."[30]

Allen wasn't certain that audiences would forgive his run-in with the law. He hoped people understood that he had learned from his mistakes and changed his lifestyle. He also hoped his show wouldn't be judged by the way he had lived his life more than a decade earlier. But he knew that it would be difficult to predict the public's reaction. His admissions about his past might go largely unnoticed, or they might doom his career.

Allen on the set of Home Improvement *during the show's first season. The engaging sitcom soon attracted a huge following.*

An Instant Hit

To Allen's relief, the public embraced his show based on its merits and didn't dwell on Allen's real-life problems. After *Home Improvement* debuted in September 1991, its audience grew steadily. Allen's drug use and prison time were forgiven as audiences fell for his amiable lout character Tim "the Toolman" Taylor. "Allen is one of the fall's freshest finds," wrote critic David Hiltbrand, who also said that the show was "relaxed and likable."[31] The series clicked with audiences as it examined the topic of men versus women in a gentle comedic fashion.

Home Improvement reached number five in the television ratings in its first season. It was the only new show of the fall 1991 TV season to be a hit. The uncertainties that had plagued Allen about his acting ability and the public's reaction to his past were erased. At thirty-eight, Allen was a television star, and by summer 1992 his popularity was sealed. He was named television's funniest actor on America's favorite sitcom, and received the first of eight consecutive People's Choice Awards for favorite male television performer. A Harris Poll named him America's favorite television personality.

On Top

Home Improvement proved it could maintain the strong momentum it had generated during its first season. The sitcom ended its second season near the top of the Nielsen ratings and was renewed for three years. This was an unusually strong show of support for a show at a time when many series were working with month-to-month contracts.

Allen had found a way to connect with audiences by tapping into what so many men wanted to do–fix something at home and make it work. The series had just the right blend of cuteness (provided by Allen's three television sons), tartness (provided by his on-screen wife, Patricia Richardson), and ineptness (provided by Allen). In 1993, Allen won a Golden Globe Award for best actor in a musical or comedy series. With its solid fan base, *Home Improvement* became the top-rated series in 1993–1994.

Mixed Blessing

Allen's success gave him the resources to pamper himself. He could now afford things he'd always wanted. However, he resisted purchasing too many luxuries. He did buy himself a Jeep and a very nice pair of binoculars but tried not to get too caught up in his fame. He knew the ratings on his show could go down as quickly as they had gone up.

Allen felt that his fame had come to him at the right time in his life. He had spent years coming up through the ranks of struggling comics, which had given him time to get his priorities straight. At thirty-nine, he had his friends, family, and social structure in place. He didn't have to worry about making friends who respected him

Familiar Face

Allen appreciated the way he and *Home Improvement* had been accepted by a national audience. He enjoyed what he was doing and was pleased that so many people could identify with the character he had created. However, the celebrity status that came with his success dramatically altered Allen's life.

Allen was now recognized wherever he went. Before his weekly television series debuted, he had enjoyed a fairly anonymous life. However, with Tim Taylor coming into living rooms across America each week, this was no longer possible. Taylor was such an easygoing, everyday kind of guy that people watching the show felt like they knew him personally. "I went to a hockey game in Detroit the other night, and there were quite a few people staring. I'd be kidding you if I said that, most of the time, it wasn't fun," Allen told Michael Leahy in *TV Guide*. "The only down side is that you give so much time to strangers, there's a lot less for your family. I hope to God I have a good handle on it."

Playing Tim Taylor put Allen in the public spotlight.

only as long as he was a television star. He had a wife and daughter who loved him, and family and friends who had stood by him as he evolved from a drifting college student into a successful television performer.

The fan base Allen had cultivated on the comedy circuit, first in the Midwest and then on the West Coast, had expanded to include families across the nation who loved the befuddled, well-meaning, overly confident handyman he played on television. Allen loved to make people laugh, and his enthusiasm was evident in the energy he devoted to his television show and the sincerity with which he played his character. However, as the demands of his career dominated his daily life, he at times envied the character he played on television. Tim Taylor was living Allen's dream life, with a nice home, loving family, just a little bit of fame, and nothing he had to think too deeply about.

Midwesterner at Heart

Although he played a dad on television and was a husband and father in real life, Allen's life at home wasn't a mirror image of the life he portrayed on television. For one thing, his daily schedule was much more cluttered than Tim Taylor's. And when he was at home, he had fewer qualms about helping out than his television counterpart did. The character he portrayed resisted anything to do with housework, other than giving the washing machine more power. In real life, Allen changed his daughter's diapers, did the dishes, and helped his wife clear the table after a meal. "I can't imagine having a marriage that works without doing that,"[32] he said.

Allen also seemed to have a better grasp on his relationship with his wife than his *Home Improvement* counterpart. In addition to helping his wife at home, he knew the value of compromise when they were away. During the 1993 summer break from his series, he took a trip to Italy with his family. His wife wanted to see famous works of art by Michelangelo and other Italian artists. He was more interested in cars, but agreed to go to museums in Florence if his wife would visit the Ferrari factory with him.

Early in his television career, Allen and his family lived in a rented home in Los Angeles. They eventually moved to Hollywood but also kept a red-brick four-bedroom ranch house in Beverly Hills,

Michigan. Allen's career was now centered in California, but he didn't want to sever his ties with the Midwest. He felt more comfortable in Michigan than he did in the Los Angeles area, where neighbors looked at him strangely when he completed the routine household chore of changing a lightbulb in the lamp along his driveway.

The Toolman, pictured with his television family, reluctantly helps with family chores. In real life, Allen actively contributes to housekeeping and child rearing.

Stifled Stand-Up

As Allen's television show became more popular, more fans saw him as the affable clean-cut dad he portrayed on television. This posed problems when it came to his stand-up routine. Onstage, Allen still enjoyed using the shockingly profane humor that had been his style before he became a television star. He talked about sex, used dirty language, and made vulgar comments. Families who came to his nightclub act expecting squeaky clean Tim Taylor instead got a dose of the earthy Tim Allen, and many weren't impressed.

Allen tried to appease both sets of fans, those who came because of his television character and those who came to see his traditional stand-up act. He cleaned up his earlier shows but still got in trouble with irate audience members. "I did San Francisco right before *Home Improvement* broke the top-five and the whole front row was, like, a Brownie troop," Allen told writer Jim Slotek of the *Toronto Sun.* "And I'm usually talking about genitals and bowel movements." He thought he was safe during the second show, but he got letters from people wondering how they were supposed to explain his sexually laced humor to their children.

Although he was grateful for the fans who loved him as Tim Taylor, Allen hated to alter his stand-up act. He loved to roll with a routine and play off the audience and didn't like censoring himself. Allen thought of the offensive words as nothing more than attention-grabbing devices and a means of making people laugh. In his view, bad words were ones that put people down, such as calling someone stupid, ugly, or fat. The words he used in his act were simply his way of punctuating his humor.

Allen, pictured with TV wife Patricia Richardson, tried to please fans of both his raunchy stand-up act and his clean-cut television character.

Replacing a lightbulb was a household chore he could handle, and he didn't mind doing it. Allen enjoyed puttering around the house when he had the chance, but had learned that he was better at talking about men's passion for tools than he was at household repairs. Like his television persona, Allen liked fixing things at home but wasn't very adept at it. "First, I'd have to get a book about what I gotta do," he said. "Then, I'd make four hours of mistakes and seven trips to the hardware store." [33]

Road to Success

While Allen realized that his skills as a handyman were limited, there seemed to be no limit as to what he could do with his career. He had successfully transferred his comedy routine to television, and he was popular with the public. It was the perfect time for him to see what else he could do with his talent.

Allen wasn't sure he wanted to do more. But executives at Disney saw how well liked he was. Allen was a bankable television star, and the studio wanted to see if his talent could be successful in other areas as well.

Allen still wanted to put in the effort necessary to keep his series on top, and realized that any addition to his workload would have an impact on his family and his personal life. It would require more time away and erase any anonymity he might still have in public. But he decided he couldn't pass up the chance to build on what he had accomplished. He wanted to see what else he could conquer.

Chapter 4

Overdrive

T IM ALLEN AND Disney were poised to take advantage of his popularity. Allen had made the jump from the stand-up stage to television. Perhaps he could make the leap from the small screen to the big screen as well.

As he had done with his television series, Allen was choosy about the project that would launch a new facet of his career. Television stars aren't always successful in movies, and Allen was still new to the acting profession. He had started as a comedian stretching his act into a half-hour television show, had won some acclaim for his ability, and was now poised to try the next step. To have a chance at success, he needed to find a script that fit his personality and suited his acting talents. When he read the script for a movie called *The Santa Clause,* he laughed out loud. He had found the vehicle that would make him a movie star.

The Santa Clause

The Santa Clause was written by two comedians Allen knew, Leo Benvenuti and Steve Rudnick. Allen played the central character, Scott Calvin, a divorced dad who struggles when it comes to connecting with his son. Their relationship is strained until Santa Claus falls off Calvin's roof on Christmas Eve. When Calvin takes on the role of St. Nick, the transformation brings him closer to his son.

The movie was produced by Disney and directed by John Pasquin, a *Home Improvement* director who was familiar with Allen's acting style. Allen had lobbied to get Pasquin as the movie's director. He wanted to be surrounded by familiar faces as he took on a new challenge.

To successfully show both the flawed and sensitive sides of his character, Allen had to learn to portray more emotions on-screen.

To help Allen show sadness in one scene, Pasquin reminded him that, while he was shooting the movie in Toronto, his four-year-old daughter and wife were hundreds of miles away in Hollywood. Allen was missing significant moments in his daughter's childhood that could never be recaptured. Allen had tried to stay in touch by sending her faxes, but that couldn't erase the sad, guilty feeling that washed over him whenever he thought about what his latest career move was doing to his family. It was a painful situation for Allen, and when Pasquin reminded him of it during shooting, Allen yelled at him afterward for bringing those feelings to the surface. However, Allen also recognized that calling up that emotion during the scene benefited the movie, and the ability to show the sadness his character felt made him a better actor.

In a scene from The Santa Clause, *Allen converses with a young girl. His high-powered career caused frequent absences from his own daughter.*

More Discomfort

Allen had to deal with more than his emotional discomfort during the shooting of the movie. Complicating matters during filming was the eighty-five-pound fat suit Allen had to wear to become Santa. The uncomfortable, hot suit took five hours to put on and two hours to take off, and gave Allen heat rash. Yet for twenty-two days of the sixty-day movie shoot, Allen had to wear the suit on a set that was so hot that some of the kids who played elves passed out. He considered wearing clothing filled with coolant under the fat suit, but that only made him shiver. Instead, to cool off between takes, he found some relief by sticking a hair dryer hose into the suit. "That Tim comes across as a jolly guy, knowing how miserable he was–that's acting!"[34] said Rudnick.

Allen wasn't making the movie in plush surroundings. The giant soundstage in Toronto accommodated the North Pole scenery but wasn't especially friendly toward the actors. It was next to a waterway, and when tugboats went by, shooting would have to stop until the noise quieted down. The movie had a rather tight budget, until Disney gave it a last-minute million-dollar boost. This provided the resources for more music and special effects, giving the final product blockbuster potential.

The film didn't turn out the way Allen had originally envisioned. When Allen read the original script, it had a dark tone, with Santa getting shot instead of falling off a roof. However, with a holiday release and family audiences in mind, Disney took out the shooting and made it more family oriented. The new version ends with Allen's character bonding with his son and coming to an understanding with his ex-wife. Allen admitted that he preferred the darker version. "I thought it was funny," Allen said. "If it was up to me, I would've left it that way."[35]

Author

Allen didn't object to the changes, however. This was his first movie, and he was going to do what it took to make it successful. He was also busy with another project. Between shooting scenes of *The Santa Clause,* Allen was writing his first book. It had been a project Disney had wanted him to do even before *Home Improvement*

Detroit Debut

Allen showed his devotion to Michigan by insisting that *The Santa Clause* have its premiere at the Fox Theatre in Detroit rather than in California. He also wanted to triumphantly return to the state where he had made his mistakes, turned his life around, and started the career that took him to stardom. Four years earlier, Allen had been a stand-up comic from Michigan. Now he was an actor on the big screen, as well as the author of a best-selling book and a television star.

Allen's parents, grandparents, and friends such as race-car drivers Mario and Michael Andretti were there to help him celebrate this new milestone. The mood was set with a red carpet, white stretch limousines, and a seven-piece band playing "Jingle Bells." "Never in my wildest imagination did I believe I'd be standing here like this one day," the forty-one-year-old Allen said in a Knight-Ridder newspaper article.

A flurry of snowflakes dusts Allen and his young costar in a scene from The Santa Clause.

premiered in 1991. After seeing tapes of his comedy act, an editor from Hyperion, Disney's publishing arm, had wanted Allen to write a book based on his comedy. However, Allen didn't want to write a book on the eve of his television debut. He was consumed with making the transition from stand-up to television comedy and didn't want to venture into yet another new area at the same time. He also knew that if he waited and his television series was a hit, his book could be an even bigger success.

After three years of great television ratings and recognition from fans, Allen agreed that the time was right for him to write a

The triple threat comic-actor-writer autographs copies of his best-selling book Don't Stand Too Close to a Naked Man.

book. But now that he had agreed to write one, he had to find the time to do so. While making *The Santa Clause,* he eked out time between scenes to write *Don't Stand Too Close to a Naked Man* in his trailer on the set. The pressure of writing his first book and making his first movie was daunting. Before writing the book, his professional writing experience consisted of one *Home Improvement* script. Allen called writing the book at the same time he was making the movie the dumbest thing he had ever done, as he realized he was more of a comedian than a writer. However, with the help of writer David Resnin, the project came together, and Allen found the writing process ultimately fulfilling. It allowed him to show readers who he was outside of television, and he came away from the writing process with renewed energy. "It helped me blow out my motors and defoul my spark plugs,"[36] he said.

Part of the reason writing the book was such a catharsis for Allen was the tack he took with the text. Disney had wanted him to write a book mainly containing humor, but Allen wanted something deeper. He had studied philosophy in college and didn't want to hide his thoughtful side. The book contains autobiographical, humorous, and philosophical elements. His goal was to have readers laugh and think at the same time. "If you come away with a smile and you like your wife a little bit better or you like your husband a little bit better, then I've accomplished something,"[37] he said.

In the book, Allen talks about his life. He discusses his boyhood war games and how he was teased as a child about his name. He also shares his feelings about the death of his father and his time in prison. But the book isn't just an autobiography. It also includes material from his comedy act, such as his take on power tools and the relationship between men and women. The title, *Don't Stand Too Close to a Naked Man,* hints at his time in prison but has little relevance to most of the material in the book. It was chosen mainly because it was funny. When Allen suggested the title during a meeting of Disney executives, people at the meeting laughed so hard they shot mineral water through their noses.

Allen's favorite parts of the book are his observations about men and women. He talks about his mother, wife, and sister. His favorite line in the book is "no matter how much trouble men are to women–and it's a lot–it's women who raise us, who form us, and so they have to take credit for what we are."[38]

Three on Top

Like his television series, Allen's book was an immediate hit. It debuted at number eleven on the *New York Times* best-seller list before he even promoted it on talk shows such as *PrimeTime Live,*

Oprah, and *Late Night with David Letterman.* Soon it topped the best-seller list. Although it was criticized as being little more than an extended comedy routine of interest mainly to Allen's fans, readers enjoyed his observations.

Allen's success as an author wasn't the only reason he was in the news that fall. *The Santa Clause* was making its debut, and would be a favorite of holiday moviegoers. The popularity Allen had had on television and as an author carried over to the movie; *The Santa Clause* made it to number one at the box office on Thanksgiving weekend in 1994. It earned $71 million in its first seventeen days. In four weeks, it brought in $84 million. *The Santa Clause* surpassed movies like *Interview with a Vampire* with Tom Cruise, *Star Trek: Generations,* and *Junior,* in which Arnold Schwarzenegger plays a pregnant man.

Allen appears in a scene from The Santa Clause, *which became a huge hit.*

Allen had been uncomfortable, homesick, and stressed during the making of *The Santa Clause,* but it didn't show on-screen as he evolved from self-absorbed executive to jolly St. Nick. He won the 1995 People's Choice Award for favorite actor in a comedy motion picture for his role as Scott Calvin/Santa Claus. He also received the Blockbuster Entertainment Award for favorite male newcomer–theatrical for the role.

Keeping It in Perspective

Allen wanted to savor the moment: He had a number-one book, movie, and television show all at the same time. Disney made a poster for him to commemorate the event. Allen saw it as a unique accomplishment, one he doubted would be duplicated. He was careful not to make too much of it, however. He knew in the long run that his accomplishment would be seen as little more than an interesting piece of trivia. "That was such a critical mass of timing; I suppose difficult to achieve, but I don't think it's the kind of thing that goes down in history," Allen said. "When I'm long gone, maybe it'll be a *Jeopardy* question."[39]

Allen's devotion to his work paid off with perks, such as the use of a private jet for his book promotion tour. Disney gave him a $66,000 Porsche, a four-wheel-drive sports car that was the perfect gift for the man who loved powerful vehicles. Allen joked that he had done so much for Disney that the corporation had bought him Guam, an island in the Pacific Ocean. "I am now the Prince of Guam, which is all I ever really wanted to do in my life," he said. "I'm carried around on those sticks and those chairs."[40]

Insecure

Allen was very happy to be on top, but he couldn't relax and enjoy his position. He waited eagerly for the weekly television ratings so that he could see how his show fared against the competition. He knew that it would one day likely fall from the top spot, and he nervously awaited the inevitable. "I know I'll go from being a sort of messiah to a pariah," he said. "That's the natural evolution of things. Something's going to happen to us. I don't know what, exactly. But it will. My job is to do everything I can to stay on top for as long as I can."[41]

On Track

Tim Allen's success in comedy gave him the resources to indulge in another passion, auto racing. In the early 1990s, Allen met Steve Saleen, the owner of Saleen, Inc. Saleen's company, based in Irvine, California, makes high-performance vehicles. Allen was performing his stand-up act in Hermosa Beach, California, when Saleen stopped by after the show and brought two cars with him for Allen to try. After taking a test drive, Allen was convinced he wanted Saleen to modify a car for him.

To build Allen's $50,000 dream car, Saleen took a Mustang and added more power. The supercharged racing car was equipped with a 575-horsepower engine. The fuel injection supercharged Ford V-8 engine could power the Mustang to 180 miles per hour.

After watching Allen drive his new car around the test track a few times, Saleen saw that the comedian and actor had the potential to be a race-car driver. One of Allen's first races was at Elkhart Lake, Wisconsin, on July 8, 1995. He finished sixth in the sports class. After the race, Allen was dehydrated and hyperventilating, but he wouldn't hear of being taken to the hospital. He wanted to savor the postrace ambiance at the track. He did have to make a trip to the hospital the next year, however, after breaking a rib when he spun and hit the wall at the Thunderdome Sports Complex in St. Petersburg, Florida.

The mishaps at the track didn't deter Allen from pursuing his interest in racing. He and Saleen formed the Saleen-Allen RRR Speedlab Racing Team, and although they have drivers in addition to Allen, he still gets behind the wheel when he can. Their team won the final race of the Sports Car Club of America (SCAA) World Challenge series in 1995, and won the SCCA Manufacturers Championship in 1996, 1997, and 1998.

Since he knew he had to make the most of his time on top, Allen felt like he couldn't rest because he didn't know when it would end. In 1995 he did the voice of Buzz Lightyear in the computer-animated film *Toy Story*. Playing opposite Tom Hanks, who was the voice of the cowboy doll Woody, Allen's self-absorbed baritone was the perfect voice for a space ranger who can't believe he's just a toy. Allen also wrote scripts and worked on a television special, and because of his success, people paid close attention to his ideas. He was unsure how long he would have that type of power, however. "Never take anything for granted," he said. "You never know if it's going to knock you down. No. Forget that. You know it's going to knock you down. You just don't know when."[42]

Strained Family Ties

The attention that Allen's career demanded meant that he had little time for his siblings and parents. His family was close-knit, and although Allen was no stranger to his home state of Michigan, he didn't always have time to go there to see his family. One June he wasn't able to make it home to celebrate his stepdad's ordination as an Episcopalian deacon, but he was able to attend the Detroit Grand Prix the next day. "You can imagine, we were very disappointed,"[43] his mother said. His mother also did not care for the jokes Allen made in his book *Don't Stand Too Close to a Naked Man* about growing up with the last name of Dick.

His fame had made Allen less accessible to his brothers and sisters. They had their own lives in other parts of the country. "The hardest thing for [his siblings] is that their brother is a little less touchable now," Allen's mother said. "He's being pulled in so many ways."[44]

Security

In September 1995, Allen was assured of financial security when *Home Improvement* went into syndication. Instead of being shown only weekly on a national network, the show could be purchased by local stations and shown on multiple nights a week. Allen shared in the revenue generated by the additional airings of the show.

Home Improvement began its Monday-through-Friday run in unprecedented style by opening with a new episode, which featured Tim and Jill visiting a military base and racing tanks. The show's popularity carried over into syndication, and *Home Improvement* became the top-rated syndicated sitcom, beating *Seinfeld, Roseanne,* and *The Simpsons.* However, having the show in syndication made it more difficult for the series to maintain its strong pull in the weekly ratings. Viewers had so many opportunities to see the syndicated show that they didn't feel as inclined to tune in to the network's weekly airing as regularly as they had in previous years. In its fifth season, Allen's fears about his series sliding in the ratings were confirmed. *Home Improvement* was the number-five or number-six show in the ratings most weeks.

Maintaining harmony on the set became more tenuous as the children in the series began to become stars in their own right. The young actors on the series, Zachery Ty Bryan, Jonathan Taylor Thomas, and Taran Noah Smith, were dealing with school, their

Allen and Richard Karn, his Home Improvement *sidekick Al. In 1995 the once invincible sitcom began to decline in the ratings.*

work on the set, magazine interviews, fan mail, and offers for other projects. The trio was aware of their popularity and impact on the show's ratings. In 1993 they had called in sick for six days because of dissatisfaction with their $8,000-per-episode paychecks. That issue had been settled with an offer of about $12,000 an episode, but it highlighted the fact that the show had to do more than satisfy audiences to be successful. It also had to pacify its cast members.

Allen tried to keep the mood on the set light, realizing that it was important for the cast to maintain its chemistry for the show to be a hit. He said that Thomas remained a sweet kid who happened to get a ton of mail, and joked, "We're not actually allowed to speak to him. You can't make eye contact with him anymore; you actually have to talk to his people."[45] After the series ended, Thomas remembered Allen's humor as the highlight of being on a television show. "The best part was being there, laughing with Tim Allen,"[46] he said.

Allen had maintained his sense of humor and quick wit as his career grew at a dizzying pace. Not content to be only a television star, Allen had branched out to other media with great success. His television show, book, and movie all made it to number one. Rather than basking in his success, however, Allen was a bit nervous living life at the top. He had enjoyed the challenge of making the climb but was afraid to settle back and enjoy the view. The pressure to stay on top was just as daunting as the ascent had been. In addition, Allen worried that now there was nowhere to go but down.

Chapter 5

Putting on the Brakes

Allen's career did not go into the free fall he feared it would. He channeled his anxiety about his fame into work on his television show, movies, and another book. He didn't keep doing exactly the same thing, however. With his movies and book, he sought to step away a bit from the bumbling, amiable Toolman he portrayed on television. There was a deeper side to Allen's personality, and he cautiously began to take steps to expose it more fully with the projects he chose. Allen couldn't shake the feelings about the temporary nature of fame, and dealt with his concerns by tapping into his philosophical side.

The result was a 1996 book titled *I'm Not Really Here*. As in his previous book, Allen combined humor and heavier material. Although it contains some information about his family, Allen's second book is less autobiographical than his first. *I'm Not Really Here* is set against the backdrop of Allen's spending a weekend at home alone, searching for a 1956 Ford hood ornament that Allen says is perfect. He discusses life as he suffers from a midlife crisis while his wife and daughter are out of town.

Some of the book's humor is derived from a weighty subject: the death of Allen's father. As he talks about how it has taken years for him to find the ability to forgive the man who killed his father, Allen puts a light spin on the dark moments. When he was a kid, he dreamed about finding the man who was driving the car that slammed into the one driven by his father. As an adult, he found humor in the impracticality of his wish. "When you're a kid there's not much you can do," he said. "You can only ride your bike so far. I don't know what we'd do if we ever caught him . . . pea shoot him to death? 'Hold him down.' 'Ow, ow!'"[47]

Written in a stream-of-consciousness style, the book is a jumbled series of loosely connected events. Allen gets advice about life from a series of people, including a FedEx deliveryman, old friends, and salesmen at car shows. He puts his midlife crisis in the context of quantum physics theories and the philosophy of Eastern religions.

Allen tries to show personal growth in the book, but its jumbled ramblings and lack of continuity make the depth Allen sought seem convoluted and forced. Because it shows another side of the comedian, however, some thought it might open him up to a broader audience. "Life, death, love, hate, existence, the universe. You won't be seeing it in a sitcom anytime soon," said reviewer Jim Slotek. "And it will probably leave a lot of *Home Improvement* fans cold. On the other hand, people who never appreciated the Toolman may like this version of Tim Allen."[48]

Tim Allen's Stops on the Way to Success

Voice of Middle America

Even though he felt it was necessary to reveal his philosophical side, Allen still saw himself as a champion of Middle America. He gave a voice to people who derived satisfaction from having a home, a family, and a great set of power tools. His show held on to a set of family values not always admired in Hollywood. "I'm not saying I'm Mr. Blue Collar, but I just appreciate some things that bypass some people here [in Hollywood]," Allen said. "That's what Tool Time started as: celebrating what men do with their hands–and women, too."[49]

As much as he appreciated the television character he had created, Allen also felt that his work in the comedy series was keeping him from exploring his acting talent further. He wanted to try a science fiction movie that didn't involve comedy, or perhaps play a villain. He hesitated, however. Comedy had made him king, and it was a genre he enjoyed. He was also unsure if audiences would accept him

The Scientific Tim Allen

On Tim Allen's website (www.timallen.com), one topic area open for discussion is quantum physics. Allen wanted to provide a place where people could exchange ideas about science, quantum physics, and spirituality. It may seem odd that a comedian is interested in the order of the universe, but dabbling in physics gives Allen the tools he needs to try to make sense of his life and his successful career.

Allen is especially interested in the particles that make up matter. He says he got lost looking at the vastness of the universe, so to try to understand the world, he wants to learn about the tiniest particles instead of the largest. His interest in physics inspired the title for his second book, *I'm Not Really Here.*

After his television show ended, Allen had an opportunity to learn more about antimatter when he toured CERN, the European Organization for Nuclear Research founded in 1954. Scientists at the research facility in Switzerland explore what matter is made of and try to discover what holds it together. Allen got to see a nuclear accelerator and thought the next phase of his career might include translating physics for the common man, using his skills as a performer. "That's what comedy is: translating pretty complex ideas in a very simple way, you know, word play," he told *Reader's Digest.* "What a thrilling idea to . . . explain what quantum mechanics, quantum physics means on this level of reality. It's daunting, but so stupid that a comedian would go, 'Yeah, okay, I'll take a shot at that.'"

In the 1996 film Jungle 2 Jungle, *Allen's character and his jungle-raised son find themselves in a bind in New York City.*

in a different role. Audiences expected Allen to entertain them in a funny manner, and he was afraid that if he altered what they expected, he would be rejected. Allen was pulled by the urge to try something different but also wanted to keep audiences happy and stay busy.

Jungle 2 Jungle

While his series was on hiatus in 1996, Allen chose to make the movie *Jungle 2 Jungle.* The light comedy that focuses on a father and son becoming reacquainted didn't take Allen far from his television character. In the movie, Allen plays Michael Cromwell, a driven New York businessman who wants to marry a self-absorbed fashion diva. But first he has to finalize his divorce with his estranged wife, who is living in the Amazon jungle. He makes his way to the jungle to see her and discovers he has a son. Cromwell is convinced to bring the boy to the concrete jungle of New York City.

Jungle 2 Jungle, a remake of the French comedy *Little Indian, Big City,* includes some lighthearted and tender moments as Allen teaches his son the ways of life in the city. Much of the humor evolves from the mistakes his son makes as he struggles to adapt to city life, such as when he urinates into a potted plant. Allen has his humorous moments as well and displays his comic timing when his character accidentally shoots a dart laced with a sleeping potion at the family cat and then into his foot. The movie offered familiar fare to Allen's fans, and although part of him wanted to try something different, Allen was drawn to the movie because of the development of the relationship between the father and son. "You can never have too many movies about fathers learning to be fathers,"[50] he said.

Although Allen's character was a familiar one, making the movie was far from easy. To film the movie, Allen traveled to South America and New York. Following the work on his television series, the movie's production schedule gave him little breathing time. He saw it as a necessity, however. "If I don't do it, maybe it won't happen again," he said. "The heat is on now—if I don't do it, will the heat go away?"[51]

New Confidant

Allen had some concerns when comedian Martin Short was cast as his costar in the movie. Short plays a high-strung business associate in *Jungle 2 Jungle*, and initially Allen feared that Short's high-energy comedy style wouldn't mesh with his brand of humor. However, John Pasquin, who had directed Allen in *Home Improvement* and *The*

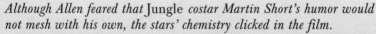

Although Allen feared that Jungle *costar Martin Short's humor would not mesh with his own, the stars' chemistry clicked in the film.*

Santa Clause, convinced him to give it a try. Pasquin was right. While the movie had other shortcomings that kept it from being a blockbuster, the pairing of Short and Allen worked well. Short held back enough to make their styles compatible and had enough scenes of his own in which to showcase his antic comedy.

More important than their on-screen work was the friendship that they developed during filming. They were able to trade one-liners, and Short was a peer Allen could confide in regarding his feelings about where his comedy and career were taking him. Short understood how fulfilling yet restricting it could be to do comedy. "Martin Short and I were talking on the set and he said: 'You have a contract with America to do a certain type of enter-tainment,'" Allen recalled. "'If you go outside that contract, they might want to revoke your license.'"[52]

The movie premiered in March 1997 at Detroit's Fox Theatre (Allen again used his clout to bring the premiere to the Midwest). He used the opening to raise money for Lighthouse of Oakland County, a human service agency for low-income families and se-niors. The movie was a modest success, grossing more than $12 million in its first weekend and eventually more than $70 million. However, critics gave Allen few accolades for portraying essen-tially the same character he had played in *The Santa Clause,* and the movie suffered from a complicated subplot involving coffee fu-tures and Russian criminals. However, families enjoyed the film's lighter moments, such as Allen convincing his son to eat Cap'n Crunch rather than pigeons and running from the giant spider his son kept as a pet. When it came out on video, the movie was the top video release its first week out.

For Richer or Poorer

For his next foray into moviemaking, Allen chose a romantic com-edy. A small step away from his divorced dad movie persona, Allen again played a self-absorbed businessman whose inner nice guy is revealed after circumstances force him to shed his material-istic values. With his on-screen wife Kirstie Alley, he gets into trou-ble with the IRS and runs from the law. Once again, Allen's character ends up in unfamiliar surroundings; the couple hides in an Amish community in rural Pennsylvania.

The movie starts slowly with some run-of-the-mill chase scenes, but there are some funny moments as the materialistic couple tries to blend in with the Amish. However, Allen and Alley never really click on-screen, although Allen manages to pull off a tender ending. *For Richer or Poorer* grossed $6 million its first weekend, opening in third place, and ended up grossing more than $31 million.

Problems with Alcohol

Allen had gone into production of *For Richer or Poorer* while on hiatus from his television show. The cycle of going from his television show to a movie to the television show and back to a movie was taxing because he didn't get a break from his hectic schedule. However, he still felt like he had to stay busy as long as he was getting movie offers. "I do have that fear that I might not work again," he said. "All this is still a little surprising to me. . . . When I was doing TV specials and selling out arenas and doing Vegas five weeks of the year, I figured that was it for me."[53]

Allen's hectic schedule gave him a sense of job security, but it also contributed to a problem that had crept into his life. Allen was drinking too much. At first he had used alcohol to wind down after a day on the set, but it eventually became his crutch. In May 1997

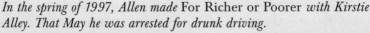

In the spring of 1997, Allen made For Richer or Poorer *with Kirstie Alley. That May he was arrested for drunk driving.*

he was arrested in Bloomfield Hills, Michigan, for driving under the influence. Allen, forty-three, was stopped for going 70 miles per hour in a 40-mile-per-hour zone. After failing a sobriety test, he was given probation, a restricted driving license, and a $500 fine.

The next May, Allen spent three weeks at an alcohol rehabilitation center as part of the plea bargain for the drunk driving arrest. In rehab, he was forced to admit that he wasn't facing his problems, including alcohol addiction and a tendency to bury himself in work. He had been addicted to staying busy and winding down with alcohol. He realized that he was constantly distracting himself with work and alcohol so that he wouldn't have to sit still and look at what his life was like. "I had a pause button during the day," Allen recalled a few years later. "All of a sudden at one part of the day, cocktail hour, I was pausing everything . . . but it's like a fake stop because the next day you've just backed up and it's twice as bad."[54]

Strained Marriage

One of the things Allen hadn't been facing was the state of his marriage. He felt guilty about being away from home so much, but that hadn't stopped him from working on a television show, writing books, and making movies. When he wasn't making movies, Allen tried to establish family routines, like starting the week by eating popcorn and watching tapes of his show with his family on Sunday nights. However, it was difficult for serene evenings at home with his family to compete with the pressure, and enjoyment, Allen's work brought him. Early in his career, Allen had been concerned that working on a television show would put additional stress on his marriage. It did, and around the time Allen was in the alcohol rehab program, rumors that his marriage was failing made it into tabloid newspapers. Allen's spokeswoman denied the rumors, but Allen admitted that he wasn't the easiest husband for a woman to have. "I cause a lot of stress in my wife's life,"[55] he said.

Financially, however, Allen was at the top of his game. In 1998 he signed a contract to earn $1.25 million per episode for *Home Improvement*. *Forbes* magazine estimated his wealth at $77 million. Allen was the best-paid comedy performer on television. Although no longer number one, his show was still rated in the top ten. But even though he had a record-setting salary and a highly rated show,

Allen wasn't satisfied. He was disappointed that his show wasn't bracketed by other hits that would have given it the support it needed to compete for the top spot. He had the money but really wanted to be on top of the ratings again. He was always second-guessing himself, thinking about how things could have been done differently to make the show a little better. It wasn't until after the series ended and he watched reruns of the show with his daughter that Allen appreciated the quality of the work he had done on the show.

End of the Road

The next year, Allen decided he had had enough. It was time to end *Home Improvement*'s eight-year run. Though he still loved the routine of going to the studio and hanging out with the cast after the episode was taped, he felt that the show had run its course. The children were getting older, and the show would have to be re-worked if it wanted to recapture the juxtaposition of adult and child attitudes that had been part of its earlier seasons. Allen knew that he had taken the show as far as it could go. "I didn't want it to end because I loved it so much—and it certainly wasn't a money issue," he said. "I just didn't want the show to tire itself out—I didn't want to have to push an old car down the road. The cast members, the crew and the staff were like a second family to me. It was the hardest decision I ever made."[56]

In January 1999, Allen received his eighth consecutive People's Choice Award for favorite male TV star, and hinted at the ceremony that this would be the series' final year. He confirmed his intentions a few days later. "When it's just about money, when it's just about ratings, it's just over," he said. "It would have been my choice to go last year."[57]

ABC executives hoped he would change his mind, but Allen and costar Richardson were firm in their resolve to make 1998–1999 the final season for the series. Allen had his eye on making more movies and hoped to patch up the family relationships he had let slide in pursuit of his career.

Star-Studded Finale

Home Improvement's final episode featured Tim quitting *Tool Time* and his wife deciding to take a new job. They couldn't quite leave

The cast of Home Improvement *is pictured here in an emotional shot following the final show.*

their comfortable life behind, however, and ended up moving their house on a barge to Indiana. Allen filled the show with guest stars as he said good-bye to the series.

To help ease the pain of filming the final show, the cast wound down with a wrap party at a stage on the Disney lot. The band Big Bad Voodoo Daddy played swing music, and everyone in the cast and crew received a *Home Improvement* class ring and yearbook as well as a designer chocolate Binford Toolbox to commemorate the show's *Tool Time* segment. Allen's costars gave him credit for keeping the show fresh and funny for so long. His team-oriented attitude and ability to keep his ego in check helped the show maintain a lighthearted quality.

New Routine

The end of Allen's television show altered his daily routine. Now he could spend more time at home with his wife and daughter, as well as pursue his interest in auto racing and producing and acting in movies. However, this change in lifestyle hurt rather than helped his marriage. Allen had truly enjoyed the routine of spending Monday through Thursday rehearsing, Friday taping, and then winding down with the cast and crew. While Allen had been absent from home due to the demands of his career, his wife had forged a different life. She had been raising their child and maintaining their home. When Allen was around more, he got in the way. Both Allen and his wife had strong wills, which sometimes led to arguments. Allen found that he had ignored his wife and daughter for too long. Laura filed for separation in November 1999.

Allen was saddened by her decision. "There are just some things in my life that I pray will remain personal," Allen said in a statement. "This is one of them. I hope that our plea for privacy during this very painful moment for my family and me will be respected."[58]

Their split came as a surprise to friends. Allen's wife and nine-year-old daughter had accompanied him to the premiere of *Toy Story 2* on November 13, in which Allen reprised his role of Buzz Lightyear, and all had appeared to be going well. "They were lifelong soulmates,"[59] said George Kutlenios, a Michigan comedy-club owner and Allen's friend.

Ending and Beginning

The end of his marriage was one in a series of changes Allen had faced over a period of a few years. He had come to terms with his dependence on alcohol and work. His television series had run its course. Now it was time for Allen to again try something new.

Allen believed that it was better to take a chance than be satisfied with mediocrity. He was in a position to take the advice he had given to Western Michigan University graduates in 1998, when he received an honorary degree from the university. "It's better to make bold choices in life, than no choices at all or even mild choices," he said. "If you're idle, you don't get anywhere."[60]

Allen had spent his career giving fans what they wanted, playing well-meaning but flawed individuals blinded by their manliness. Now he was ready to take his career in new directions. But first he had to figure out what they were.

Chapter 6

Changing Gears

Tɪᴍ Aʟʟᴇɴ ʜᴀᴅ achieved success as a comedian, actor, and author. His career was moving along at a steady pace, but he was unsure that he could top what he had already done. Allen's next challenge was to decide which direction his life should take. He now had more flexibility and more time, but he had to determine what to pursue next.

A series of health problems underscored Allen's desire to make his life more fulfilling, and caused him to reevaluate his personal and professional priorities. In October 1999, Allen underwent emergency surgery to have his appendix removed. In 2001, he was in a race car accident and ripped part of his stomach, which led to a colon infection. He eventually required surgery and had part of his intestine removed.

Allen's illness forced him to think about the impermanence of the good life. "All this stuff could go away so fast," he said. "And it all is just so temporary. And what is important becomes tantamount to everything, really what's important. And helping other people, making friends, [spending] time with [my] daughter, being kind to people. I don't know, some of these things start to make a lot more sense now." [61]

Family Matters

While his health problems made him reconsider the things he valued in life, Allen was facing his challenges head-on. He realized that much of his energy had been spent avoiding his problems or uncomfortable situations he didn't want to deal with. By staying occupied, he hadn't had to think about what other people in his life were going through. It was easier for him to react to situations than lay the groundwork for making things happen. He now faced his failures and successes rather than finding diversions to avoid them.

Although he and his wife were separated, Allen didn't distance himself from her. They still ran their charitable foundation, the Laura Deibel and Tim Allen Foundation, together. The separation was still difficult and painful for Allen, however, especially in light of the fact that professionally he projected the image of a loving family man. "My wife and I both worked hard at this and there's no easy way out of this," he said. "There's no comfortable way out of this, and it just continues. It's a process and it really is such a personal thing, it seems cheap to talk about it." [62]

Allen tried to connect with his daughter and help her make the right decisions in her life. He didn't want her to make the same mistakes with drugs that he had. Allen also quit smoking and warned his daughter about the addictive habit, saying, "It was harder to stop cigarette smoking than anything else I've ever done." [63]

Thoughts of his family made Allen want to be closer to his brothers and sisters. Allen realized how important they were to him. On past visits with his brothers, his know-it-all side had come out at times and he had offered unwanted advice. He no longer tried to change how they lived but accepted his brothers for who they were. His family leaned more toward pessimism than optimism, and he learned to accept that. "We're more of a half-empty family rather than half-full. And it prepares you for disaster really well," he said. "I've seen some other families polarized over death, illness, crime, the typical things that happen to families—that have torn other families apart. Where my family may not be the closest family, I mean, not a lot of huggin' and kissin', but we've survived a lot of things and nothing really changed." [64]

As he neared fifty, Allen realized how much he still had to learn about life. Far from the know-it-all kid who wisecracked his way through high school and college, he now appreciated what his family had taught him and knew when to keep his opinions to himself. "I don't think you know anything until you're 50," he said. "At least now I know . . . to listen more. I still don't listen enough. I know now not to tell my parents what to do. I know now to accept people more." [65]

Tools for Charity

In the mid-1990s, Tim Allen and his wife met actor Paul Newman at a car race. They admired how the star had created a line of food products and gave the profits to charity. Allen and his wife decided to develop a similar project: selling power tools to raise money for charity.

Allen and his wife consulted with toolmakers, inventors, and designers before coming up with product lines for Tim Allen Signature Tools and Tim Allen Signature Stuff. The tools, for consumers as well as professional carpenters, include a Nack Knife with fifteen blades and optional holster. The Signature Stuff collection is designed to promote creativity in kids and includes building projects for children to make with their parents, such as a folding photo frame and rain gauge.

The profits from Allen's product lines are donated to charities such as Big Brothers/Big Sisters, the Special Olympics, Toys for Tots, the Salvation Army, the American Red Cross, and the YMCA. Allen and his wife also donate money through their charitable foundation, the Laura Deibel and Tim Allen Foundation, which was established in 1992. Through the foundation they have helped the William Booth Legal Aid Clinic of the Salvation Army in Detroit, Lighthouse of Oakland County, and Forgotten Harvest in Michigan, among others. To help victims of the September 11 terrorist attack, Allen auctioned off his 1955 Chevy Nomad, which had been featured on *Home Improvement,* for the September 11/Twin Towers Fund.

Inspired by actor Paul Newman, Allen donates the profits from his product lines to charity.

Lighthearted Entertainment

Allen showed no hint of personal troubles on-screen, and for his first post–*Home Improvement* forays into film he stuck with roles he felt comfortable with. In 1999's *Toy Story 2*, released just before the announcement of his separation, Allen reprised the role of Buzz Lightyear. The digitally animated movie again followed the adventures of the toys in the room of a boy named Andy. This time, Buzz and his friends must find a way to save Woody from being shipped to a museum in Japan by a greedy toy collector. An all-star cast of vocal actors and top-notch animation brought both tenderness and humor to the characters and made the sequel even better than its well-crafted predecessor. *Toy Story 2* grossed more than $250 million, and in 2000 Allen won an Annie Award for his voice work as Buzz Lightyear.

That year Allen also did Buzz's voice for the feature-length cartoon *Buzz Lightyear of Star Command: The Adventure Begins*. Animated in traditional hand-drawn form, rather than the three-dimensional digital animation of the movies, the video centers on Buzz's battle against the evil Zurg instead of his adventures with

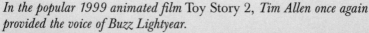

In the popular 1999 animated film Toy Story 2, *Tim Allen once again provided the voice of Buzz Lightyear.*

The 1999 spoof Galaxy Quest *allowed Allen (center, right) to fulfill his dream of making a science fiction movie.*

Woody and his friends. The cartoon was enjoyable fare for children but lacked the depth that made the *Toy Story* movies captivating for adults as well. The video served as a starting point for a *Buzz Lightyear* Saturday morning cartoon series, but Allen opted to leave the voice work for that project to actor Patrick Warburton.

Galaxy Quest

Allen next fulfilled his goal of making a science fiction film with *Galaxy Quest*. Not exactly a serious look at the future, the spoof parodies *Star Trek,* its devoted fans, and conventions. Allen had fun with his role as Jason Nesmith, an egotistical actor who had been the star of a popular science fiction series. He and his crew make a living making appearances and signing autographs for their fans. His self-centered character is forced to use his true leadership qualities when a real group of aliens asks for his assistance.

The movie benefited from well-crafted special effects and a cast that included Sigourney Weaver and Alan Rickman. It did better at the box office than expected, opening at $7 million but eventually grossing more than $70 million. Allen won a Saturn Award for best actor for his portrayal of Nesmith.

New Material

Although these movies provided Allen with some box office success, they didn't really allow him to add range to his abilities the way he wanted to. Instead, the first chances Allen took with his career came in the medium that had been his first taste of the entertainment industry: stand-up comedy. Allen made some changes to his comedy act, getting away from tools and instead making fun of other topics in his life. He wanted something fresh and decided that, although they had been painful, his health problems could be turned into something funny. "It took so long coming up with the Toolman and all that grunting, but I've kind of moved on in my head,"[66] he said.

Allen realized how much he had missed being onstage when he returned to the Just for Laughs Comedy Festival in Montreal in July 2000. A man in the front row at Club Soda in Montreal had sat glumly with his arms crossed while other comics performed. It was Allen's goal to get him laughing. He played to him during the entire show and was rewarded when the man laughed so hard his sides seemed to be hurting.

Allen still loved being onstage, but his popularity made it difficult for him to judge how funny he was by the audience's reaction. "I can stand onstage [now] and wave my arms and the audience will laugh," he said. "It's kind of a handicap. I don't know if I'm really being funny."[67]

Same Values, New Goals

Even though he no longer had to work as hard as he once did for applause from an audience, Allen didn't think of himself as any different than the person he was when he was starting out in comedy. He didn't have the same day-to-day struggles he did when he was living paycheck to paycheck, but inside he still had the same values he had when he was a struggling comic. He was kind to others and loved to make people laugh. However, instead of focusing only on making other people happy, Allen was ready to do what was best for him.

For years Allen had done the comedic work others wanted him to do, and was well compensated for it, but it hadn't always been what he wanted for himself. It was time for him to make his own life better, rather than worrying that his success would disappear if he stopped saying "yes" to projects. "I've always been a facilitator. I like making other people comfortable and happy at the expense of my own happiness," he said. "The problem is in the past I would build up resentment and let it fester, so it was really unhealthy."[68]

Different Characters

In the back of his mind, Allen knew there was another entertainment honor he could aspire to. He had won Golden Globe, People's Choice, and Kid's Choice Awards. But he had never won an Academy Award. As long as winning an Oscar was a possibility, the competitive Allen was going to continue to work on his film career.

Allen was ready to tackle roles that were very different from what he had done in the past. He didn't worry about how he would be accepted by audiences. He simply wanted to see how far he could take his acting talent.

In the summer of 2000, Allen took on the role of a hit man in *Who Is Cletis Tout?* Acting opposite Christian Slater, who plays an escaped convict, Allen has a serious role as a character who kills three people. However, the sight of Allen the family man committing murder didn't sit well with test audiences, who kept waiting for the punch line. The film's release was delayed as its producers tried to put the right spin on the film through editing. Allen blamed himself for the audience's confusion. "It's a great little film . . . but it could get lost because of my TV image,"[69] he said.

Allen tried a different kind of comedy in the movie *Big Trouble,* which was filmed in the fall of 2000. In the movie, Allen plays a divorced Miami dad who is trying to connect with his teenage son. Based on a novel by humorist and newspaper columnist Dave Barry, the film revolves around a suitcase containing a bomb and how it impacts those who happen to handle it. Allen led a large acting ensemble that included Janeane Garofalo, Patrick Warburton, and rapper Dwight (Heavy D) Myers.

Director Barry Sonnenfeld had tight control over the way Allen's character reacted in the movie. He did not want Allen to be funny in his usual way, delivering punch lines and accenting them with appropriate facial expressions. He wanted to put him in situations that were funny and have the audience laugh at the situation. This technique had worked for Sonnenfeld in the successful *Men in Black* and its sequel, and he wanted to use that style with Allen. To Sonnenfeld, it was funny when actors talked quickly and repeated the same joke, such as saying deadpan, "Was that a goat?" when a goat wanders in. The laughs came out of the actors' reactions to odd situations.

Allen took Sonnenfeld's acting advice, and they became friends during the filming of the movie, but the film didn't do well at the box office when it opened in spring 2002. It quickly faded from theaters. Its broad slapstick didn't connect with audiences who expected something different from Allen, who came across more as a loser than a tenderhearted dad. It also made fun of airport security and airplane hijacking, which were sensitive issues less than a year after the September 11, 2001, terrorist attacks.

Back to Basics

After flirting with different roles, Allen agreed to return to the type of comedy that had made him a box office success. He signed on to do a sequel to *The Santa Clause*. A sequel had been proposed shortly after the 1994 movie was established as a hit, but Allen, busy with his television show, book, and other movie offers at the time, had declined. Now, however, he was willing to give it a try.

Allen wasn't desperately trying to put his name back at the top of a list of box office hits, however. He again was choosy about how the movie was done. When the script wasn't to his liking, he asked for a rewrite that delayed production of the movie for a year.

After *The Santa Clause* sequel was delayed, Allen again teamed up with director John Pasquin for a movie that allowed him to play a familiar character in a more dramatic style. In *Joe Somebody,* which was filmed in Minnesota in the spring and summer of 2001, Allen plays a single dad in a tedious job who is picked on by the office bully. When he is humiliated in front of his daughter, he resolves to do something about it. The movie relied on a tried-and-true Allen formula—a likable but flawed ordinary guy who finds that he has the ability to make a difference. Allen realized that the

Allen appears in a scene from the 2000 comedy Big Trouble. *The film offered a new challenge for Allen.*

movie wouldn't have a heavy meaning but was drawn to it because it had a heart. "I like stories where your heart beats a little deeper," he said. "The best episodes of *Home Improvement* had it–and then cut to me being hit in the head with a hammer."[70]

The movie also contained dramatic elements that appealed to Allen. Rather than taking on the role of a self-confident, egotistical character, Allen played a geek who dressed in dorky clothes and had a meek attitude. Eager to play a character somewhat outside the typical Allen mold, he enjoyed tackling a role that was meatier than other parts he had played. He realized that he was taking a chance with the movie because it didn't contain as much comedy as audiences would expect from him, but it was an opportunity for him to grow as an actor. "This is a much darker movie and more in tune with what is going on in Tim's own life," Pasquin said. "His divorce has definitely made him a darker person and he's now into year three of Alcoholics Anonymous and there's a lot of old pent-up

Bruising Work

Making *Joe Somebody* brought some physically uncomfortable moments for Allen. In the movie he learns self-defense from a struggling martial arts master, played by Jim Belushi. In real life, Belushi and Allen worked with fight coordinator Damon Caro, who had also worked with Brad Pitt in *Fight Club,* and was intent on making the scenes realistic. Allen ended up with so many bruises on his arms and legs from the punches that they couldn't be hidden with makeup. In the later scenes in the gym, Allen was covered with pads to hide the bruises.

The busy actor attends the premiere of his 2001 film Joe Somebody.

anger coming out, but it's made Tim far more grounded."[71] In one scene, Joe tries to ignore his troubles by turning to alcohol, going on a drinking bender for a week. Allen was able to make the scene believable because he could draw on the personal experiences he had before he joined Alcoholics Anonymous.

Joe Somebody was not a significant force at the box office when it was released in December 2001, but it gave Allen a chance to do something a little different with his acting and find an artistic outlet to deal with some of his recent personal troubles. The movie was criticized for being too sentimental and predictable, but it also had some good moments and silly fun. One reviewer said Allen's acting was the best thing about the film. "Allen seems to personify 'relaxing into character,'" said Scott Foundas. "Watching him puts you at ease."[72]

Learning Curve

Allen had been in the entertainment business for twenty years, and had achieved success in television, movies, and print. At times, however, the degree of his success still surprised Allen. He knew he would have a difficult time topping his past accomplishments in the entertainment field, but the desire to do more on the big screen still fueled his competitive juices.

Allen was aware that success in future movies was anything but certain. However, he was confident that there was one area where he could set goals and reach them: his personal life. He could control how he treated others and himself. "If success means better than the last time, then I can't do that, but if success means a bigger heart and a more glorious expression of me, then I can possibly do that because there's a lot more that I can do, now that I'm a nicer guy," he said. "Or not a nicer guy, but I'm easier on myself. I'm a much nicer guy to myself."[73]

Allen realized he had to stop judging himself by standards that were too high and needed to let himself enjoy what he had accomplished. Deep down, he was still the same guy who had been struggling on the comedy circuit. "Tim Allen? No, I'm still Tim Dick, the wisecracking kid from the upper Midwest, looking for answers to life's big questions," he said. "I'm just fortunate to be

Having grown personally and as an actor, Allen recognizes the value of keeping his life and his career in balance.

able to create as much as I do and have people like it. I just worked hard enough–and was lucky enough to become the owner of a red-hot franchise called 'Tim Allen.'" [74]

Allen realizes he doesn't have all the insights and answers to life's quirks. But it fascinates him to keep looking. And it's not in his nature to back away from a challenge.

Notes

Introduction: Toolin' Around

1. Quoted in E! Online, "Q & A with Tim Allen," n.d. www.eonline.com.
2. Quoted in E! Online, "Q & A with Tim Allen."

Chapter 1: Starts and Stops

3. Tim Allen, *Don't Stand Too Close to a Naked Man.* New York: Hyperion, 1994, p. 21.
4. Allen, *Don't Stand Too Close to a Naked Man,* p. 33.
5. Quoted in Jeff Rovin, "Tim Allen's Merry Christmas," *Ladies Home Journal,* December 1992, p. 44.
6. Quoted in *Reader's Digest,* "Our Uncut Interview with Tim Allen," October 2001. www.rd.com.
7. Allen, *Don't Stand Too Close to a Naked Man,* p. 40.
8. Allen, *Don't Stand Too Close to a Naked Man,* dedication.
9. Quoted in Susan Schindehette, "Real Men Laugh Last," *People Weekly,* July 6, 1992, p. 105.
10. Quoted in Schindehette, "Real Men Laugh Last," p. 105.
11. Quoted in Michael Leahy, "Caution: Man Working . . . to Spruce up His Image," *TV Guide,* November 9, 1991, p. 8.
12. Quoted in Chris Connelly, "Broken Home: Tim Allen Didn't Have the Tool to Fix His Childhood Tragedy–Until Now," *Ladies Home Journal,* April 1997, p. 46.

Chapter 2: Revving Up

13. Quoted in Schindehette, "Real Men Laugh Last," p. 105.
14. Quoted in *Biography Resource Center.* Farmington Hills, MI: Gale Group, 2001. http://galenet.galegroup.com.

15. Quoted in Rovin, "Tim Allen's Merry Christmas," p. 44.

16. Quoted in Leahy, "Caution: Man Working . . . to Spruce up His Image," p. 8.

17. Quoted in Associated Press, "Judge Says He Saw Allen's Comedic Potential Ages Ago," March 19, 1999. www.freep.com.

18. Quoted in Leahy, "Caution: Man Working . . . to Spruce up His Image," p. 8.

19. Quoted in Richard Zoglin, "Tim at the Top: With a No. 1 Movie, a No. 1 TV Show, and a No. 1 Book, Tim Allen Is Having an Unbeatable Year," *Time,* December 12, 1994, p. 76.

20. Quoted in Rovin, "Tim Allen's Merry Christmas," p. 44.

21. Quoted in Rovin, "Tim Allen's Merry Christmas," p. 44.

22. Quoted in Zoglin, "Tim at the Top," p. 76.

23. Quoted in Zoglin, "Tim at the Top," p. 76.

24. Quoted in Zoglin, "Tim at the Top," p. 76.

25. Quoted in Rovin, "Tim Allen's Merry Christmas," p. 44.

Chapter 3: Cruising

26. Quoted in Russell Miller, "Home for the Holidays: Tim Allen," *Ladies Home Journal,* December 1993, p. 112.

27. Quoted in Rovin, "Tim Allen's Merry Christmas," p. 44.

28. Quoted in Zoglin, "Tim at the Top," p. 76.

29. Quoted in Leahy, "Caution: Man Working . . . to Spruce up His Image," p. 8.

30. Quoted in Schindehette, "Real Men Laugh Last," p. 105.

31. David Hiltbrand, *"Home Improvement," People Weekly,* September 23, 1991, p. 15.

32. Quoted in Andrew Abrahams, "Hollywood Handyman," *Ladies Home Journal,* February 1991, p. 46.

33. Quoted in Abrahams, "Hollywood Handyman," p. 46.

Chapter 4: Overdrive

34. Quoted in Tim Appelo, "Sleighing 'em: TV's Mr. Fixit Tim Allen Retools His Talents to Fill up the Big Screen as Jolly St. Nick in 'The Santa Clause,'" *Entertainment Weekly,* November 18, 1994, p. 20.

35. Quoted in Appelo, "Sleighing 'em," p. 20.

36. Quoted in Appelo, "Sleighing 'em," p. 20.

37. Quoted in Marc Gunther, "Tim Allen Conquers a New Field with a Best-Selling Book," Knight-Ridder/Tribune News Service, October 6, 1994.

38. Quoted in Erica Kornberg, "Tools of the Trade," *Entertainment Weekly,* September 30, 1994, p. 52.
39. "Biography," Tim Allen's official website, www.timallen.com.
40. Quoted in Mike Duffy, "King of Comedy's Crown Rests Lightly on Tim Allen," Knight-Ridder/Tribune News Service, January 15, 1996.
41. Quoted in Michael Blowen, "Comedian/Author Tim Allen Finds It's Tough Staying on Top," Knight-Ridder/Tribune News Service, October 19, 1994.
42. Quoted in Blowen, "Comedian/Author Tim Allen Finds It's Tough Staying on Top."
43. Quoted in Zoglin, "Tim at the Top," p. 76.
44. Quoted in Zoglin, "Tim at the Top," p. 76.
45. Quoted in Duffy, "King of Comedy's Crown Rests Lightly on Tim Allen."
46. Quoted in Tom Gliatto and Alison Singh Gee, "Smart Throb: *Home Improvement*'s Jonathan Taylor Thomas, 18, Prepares for College," *People Weekly,* January 31, 2000, p. 107.

Chapter 5: Putting on the Brakes

47 Quoted in Connelly, "Broken Home," p. 46.
48. Jim Slotek, "Angst of a Sitcom Star," April 27, 1997. www.canoe.ca.
49. Quoted in Connelly, "Broken Home," p. 46.
50. Quoted in John Coulbourn, "The Heat Is On," March 9, 1997. www.canoe.ca.
51. Quoted in Coulbourn, "The Heat Is On."
52. Quoted in Anika Van Wyk, "Jungle Fever," March 2, 1997. www.canoe.ca.
53. Quoted in Bob Thompson, "Laughing All the Way to the Bank," December 7, 1997. www.canoe.ca.
54. Quoted in *Reader's Digest,* "Our Uncut Interview with Tim Allen."
55. Quoted in *Reader's Digest,* "Our Uncut Interview with Tim Allen."
56. Quoted in "Biography," Tim Allen's official website, www.timallen.com.
57. Quoted in Mike Duffy, "Tim Allen Insists *Home Improvement* Is All Over," January 15, 1999. www.freep.com.

58. Quoted in Mr. Showbiz, "Tim Allen's Wife Files for Separation," November 18, 1999. http://movies.go.com.

59. Quoted in Karen S. Schneider, "Home Wreck: The Foundation Beneath Tim Allen's 15-Year Marriage Crumbles," *People Weekly,* December 6, 1999, p. 81.

60. Quoted in Associated Press, "Tim Allen Gets Honorary Degree," June 29, 1998.

Chapter 6: Changing Gears

61. Quoted in *Reader's Digest,* "Our Uncut Interview with Tim Allen."

62. Quoted in *Reader's Digest,* "Our Uncut Interview with Tim Allen."

63. Quoted in *Reader's Digest,* "Our Uncut Interview with Tim Allen."

64. Quoted in *Reader's Digest,* "Our Uncut Interview with Tim Allen."

65. Quoted in *Reader's Digest,* "Our Uncut Interview with Tim Allen."

66. Quoted in Mike Duffy, "Comedian Gears up for Hometown Fans," July 15, 2001. www.freep.com.

67. Quoted in Duffy, "Comedian Gears up for Hometown Fans."

68. Quoted in Louis B. Hobson, "Making Life Improvements," December 17, 2001. www.calgarysun.com.

69. Quoted in Hobson, "Making Life Improvements."

70. Quoted in Jeff Strickler, "Tim Allen Feeling Nice About Minnesota," December 21, 2001. www.startribune.com.

71. Quoted in Hobson, "Making Life Improvements."

72. Scott Foundas, *"Joe Somebody,"* Variety, December 17, 2001, p. 36.

73. Quoted in Reader's Digest, "Our Uncut Interview with Tim Allen."

74. Quoted in "Biography," Tim Allen's official website, www.tim allen.com.

Important Dates in the Life of Tim Allen

1953

Timothy Allen Dick is born in Denver, Colorado, on June 13.

1964

Gerald Dick, Allen's father, is killed in an automobile accident.

1966

Martha Dick remarries.

1967

The family moves to Michigan.

1971

After graduating from Seaholm High School, Allen attends Central Michigan University.

1973

Allen transfers to Western Michigan University after his sophomore year at Central.

1976

Allen graduates from Western Michigan University with a degree in communications, specializing in radio and television production.

1978

Allen is arrested after trying to make a drug deal with an undercover agent at the Kalamazoo Airport.

1979

While waiting to be sentenced on drug charges, Allen begins doing stand-up comedy; he is sentenced to eight years in prison and

begins serving time at Sandstone Federal Correctional Institution
in Minnesota.

1981

Allen leaves prison and begins serving five years of parole; he
restarts his comedy career.

1984

In front of a group of tire executives in Akron, Ohio, Allen begins
making jokes about power tools and finds his comedy niche; Allen
marries Laura Deibel.

1988

The television special *Comedy's Dirtiest Dozen* includes Allen's act.

1990

Allen's comedy routine is taped for a Showtime special, *Tim Allen:
Men Are Pigs;* Allen comes to the attention of Disney executives,
who want to develop a sitcom for him; daughter Kate is born.

1991

Home Improvement begins its eight-year run on ABC; *Tim Allen Rewires
America* is shown on Showtime.

1994

Allen has the number-one movie, television show, and book all at
the same time: The role of Scott Calvin in *The Santa Clause* gives him
the top movie of the holiday season; *Don't Stand Too Close to a Naked
Man* reaches the top of the best-seller list; and *Home Improvement* is
the top-rated television series.

1995

Allen is the voice of Buzz Lightyear in the digitally animated *Toy
Story.*

1996

I'm Not Really Here, Allen's second book, is published.

1997

Jungle 2 Jungle and *For Richer or Poorer* are released; Allen plays a
self-centered but soft-hearted dad and a materialistic but loving
husband, respectively; in May, Allen is stopped for drunk driving.

1998

In May, Allen enters an alchol rehabilitation program.

1999

Home Improvement ends its eight-year run in May; in November, Allen's wife files for separation; he reprises the role of Buzz Lightyear in *Toy Story 2* and plays actor Jason Nesmith in the science fiction spoof *Galaxy Quest*.

2000

Allen does the voice for the title character in the cartoon *Buzz Lightyear of Star Command*.

2001

In *Joe Somebody,* Allen plays a wimp picked on by the office bully.

2002

Allen departs from his standard character in *Big Trouble* and *Who Is Cletis Tout?* but returns to his successful formula with another turn as Santa Claus in *Santa Clause 2: The Mrs. Clause.*

For Further Reading

Books

Michael Arkush, *Tim Allen Laid Bare*. New York: Avon Books, 1995. An in-depth biography of Allen, detailing his childhood and career through the mid-1990s.

John F. Wukovits, *Tim Allen*. Philadelphia: Chelsea House, 1999. A biography of Allen for children grade six and up that focuses on how Allen turned his life around after being arrested for selling cocaine.

Periodicals

Michael Leahy, "Caution: Man Working . . . to Spruce up His Image," *TV Guide,* November 9, 1991. In an interview early in his television career, Allen talks about the decision to come forward with information about his drug dealing and time in prison. He also discusses the dramatic difference his popular television show has already made in his life.

Joe Rusz, "Saleen R-R-R Mustang: True to His Sitcom Persona, Tim Allen Gives His Mustang a Dose of *Home Improvement*," *Road and Track,* June 1994; C. Van Tune, "Tim Allen's Wild Ride," *Motor Trend,* February 1997. Allen's passion for racing comes across as he talks about his modified Impala SS and his Saleen Mustang.

Richard Zoglin, "Tim at the Top: With a No. 1 Movie, a No. 1 TV Show, and a No. 1 Book, Tim Allen Is Having an Unbeatable Year," *Time,* December 12, 1994. The article captures Allen's pragmatic view of life at the top and discusses how he got there.

Internet Source

Reader's Digest, "Our Uncut Interview with Tim Allen," October 2001. www.rd.com. Allen discusses his family, sobriety, and thoughts on life in this interview presented in question-and-answer format. A good source for Allen's views in his own words.

Websites

Saleen Inc. (www.saleen.com). Information about Saleen/Allen Speedlab Racing.

Tim Allen's official website (www.timallen.com). Allen's website includes news about his work in movies, television, and books. There is also an idea exchange where fans can post messages about cars, movies, physics, books, and design.

Tim Allen Tools (www.timallenrrr.com). The place to learn about or buy Tim Allen Signature Tools and Tim Allen Signature Stuff.

Works Consulted

Books

Tim Allen, *Don't Stand Too Close to a Naked Man*. New York: Hyperion, 1994.

———, *I'm Not Really Here*. New York: Hyperion, 1996.

Peridicals

Andrew Abrahams, "Hollywood Handyman," *Ladies Home Journal*, February 1991.

Tim Appelo, "Sleighing 'em: TV's Mr. Fixit Tim Allen Retools His Talents to Fill up the Big Screen as Jolly St. Nick in 'The Santa Clause,'" *Entertainment Weekly*, November 18, 1994.

———, "Tim Allen," *Entertainment Weekly*, December 30, 1999.

Tim Appelo and Anne Thompson, "Santa Cruiser," *Entertainment Weekly*, December 16, 1994.

Gary Arnold, "Ho ho hot . . . Santa Suits up for the Season," *Insight on the News*, December 19, 1994.

Associated Press, "Tim Allen Gets Honorary Degree," June 29, 1998.

Michael Blowen, "Comedian/Author Tim Allen Finds It's Tough Staying on Top," Knight-Ridder/Tribune News Service, October 19, 1994.

Frank Bruni and Carol Teegardin, "Tim Allen Remembers His Roots by Opening His New Movie in Detroit," Knight-Ridder/Tribune News Service, November 10, 1994.

Alan Carter, "Good Times for Tim Allen," *Entertainment Weekly,* July 17, 1992.

Chris Connelly, "Broken Home: Tim Allen Didn't Have the Tool to Fix His Childhood Tragedy–Until Now," *Ladies Home Journal,* April 1997.

Mike Duffy, "King of Comedy's Crown Rests Lightly on Tim Allen," Knight-Ridder/Tribune News Service, January 15, 1996.

Scott Foundas, *"Joe Somebody," Variety,* December 17, 2001.

Shirliey Fung, "Arrested," *Entertainment Weekly,* June 13, 1997.

Tom Gliatto and Alison Singh Gee, "Smart Throb: *Home Improvement*'s Jonathan Taylor Thomas, 18, Prepares for College," *People Weekly,* January 31, 2000.

Marc Gunther, "Tim Allen Conquers a New Field with a Best-Selling Book," Knight-Ridder/Tribune News Service, October 6, 1994.

David Hiltbrand, *"Home Improvement," People Weekly,* September 23, 1991.

Glenn Kenny, *"The Santa Clause," Entertainment Weekly,* October 20, 1995.

Erica Kornberg, "Tools of the Trade," *Entertainment Weekly,* September 30, 1994.

Russell Miller, "Home for the Holidays: Tim Allen," *Ladies Home Journal,* December 1993.

Eric Mink, "ABC Won't Be Nailed Down on Future of *Home Improvement,"* Knight-Ridder/Tribune News Service, January 12, 1999.

Jeff Rovin, "Tim Allen's Merry Christmas," *Ladies Home Journal,* December 1992.

Leah Rozen, *"Jungle 2 Jungle," People Weekly,* March 24, 1997.

Susan Schindehette, "Real Men Laugh Last," *People Weekly,* July 6, 1992.

Karen S. Schneider, "Home Wreck: The Foundation Beneath Tim Allen's 15-Year Marriage Crumbles," *People Weekly,* December 6, 1999.

Lisa Schwarzbaum, "Dade or Alive: Director Barry Sonnenfeld and Writer Dave Barry Team up with Mixed Results in Tim Allen's *Big Trouble*," *Entertainment Weekly*, April 12, 2002.

———, "Second That Emotion: A Rare Sequel That Lives up to Its Predecessor, the Blissful *Toy Story 2* Makes You Feel as Giddy as When You First Thrilled to the Adventures of Woody and Buzz," *Entertainment Weekly*, December 3, 1999.

Mike Tribby, *"Don't Stand Too Close to a Naked Man," Booklist*, October 1, 1994.

Ken Tucker, *"Home Improvement," Entertainment Weekly*, May 21, 1993.

C. Van Tune, "Tim Allen's Wild Ride," *Motor Trend*, February 1997.

Jeffrey Wells, "Clause and Effect," *Entertainment Weekly*, January 27, 1995.

Internet Sources

Associated Press, "Judge Says He Saw Allen's Comedic Potential Ages Ago," March 19, 1999. www.freep.com.

Biography Resource Center. Farmington Hills, MI: Gale Group, 2001. http://galenet.galegroup.com.

John Coulbourn, "The Heat Is On," March 9, 1997. www.canoe.ca.

Mike Duffy, "Comedian Gears up for Hometown Fans," July 15, 2001. www.freep.com.

———, "Leaving 'Home,'" May 23, 1999. www.freep.com.

———, "Tim Allen Insists *Home Improvement* Is All Over," January 15, 1999. www.freep.com.

E! Online, "Q & A with Tim Allen," n.d. www.eonline.com.

Grand American Road Racing Association News, "Tim Allen Hot Laps Team Saleen Mustang," April 21, 2000. www.grand-am.com.

"He's No Jokester at Track," August 12, 1996. www.detnews.com.

Louis B. Hobson, "Making Life Improvements," December 17, 2001. www.calgarysun.com.

Bruce Kirkland, "Big Disappointment," n.d. www.canoe.ca.

———, "Getting the Last Laugh," April 3, 2002. www.calgarysun.com.

Louise Knott, "Tim Allen Gives Legal Aid Fund $250,000," March 15, 2000. http://detnews.com.

Mr. Showbiz, "Tim Allen's Wife Files for Separation," November 18, 1999. http://movies.go.com.

Jim Slotek, "Angst of a Sitcom Star," April 27, 1997. www.canoe.ca.

———, "Tim Sharpens His Tools," July 25, 2000. www.canoe.ca.

Jeff Strickler, "Tim Allen Feeling Nice About Minnesota," December 21, 2001. www.startribune.com.

Bob Thompson, "Laughing All the Way to the Bank," December 7, 1997. www.canoe.ca.

Anika Van Wyk, "Jungle Fever," March 2, 1997. ww.canoe.ca.

Index

Picture Credits

About the Author

Terri Dougherty is a freelance writer from Appleton, Wisconsin. In addition to nonfiction books for children, she also writes magazine and newspaper articles. A native of Black Creek, Wisconsin, Terri graduated from Seymour High School and the University of Wisconsin-Oshkosh. She was a reporter and editor at the *Oshkosh Northwestern* daily newspaper for five years before beginning her freelance writing career. In her spare time, Terri plays soccer and reads. She enjoys cross-country skiing and attending plays with her husband, Denis, and swimming, biking, and playing with their three children, Kyle, Rachel, and Emily.